The Tradition of Natural Law

The Tradition of Natural Law

A Philosopher's Reflections

by

Yves R. Simon

edited by

Vukan Kuic

with an Introduction by

Russell Hittinger

FORDHAM UNIVERSITY PRESS • NEW YORK

Library of Congress Cataloging-in-Publication Data

Simon, Yves René Marie. 1903–1961.
  The tradition of natural law : a philosopher's reflections / Yves R.
Simon : edited by Vukan Kuic : with an introduction by Russell
Hittinger.
    p.   cm.
  Originally published: 1965.
  Includes bibliographical references and index.
  ISBN 0-8232-0641-6 (pbk.) : $19.95
  1. Natural law.   I. Kuic, Vukan.   II. Title.
K428.S56   1992
340'.112—dc20   92-5480
                                                           CIP

Printed in the United States of America

Contents

PART TWO

Foreword

It is civilization which makes life with other men in society tolerable and which provides individuals with the opportunities to realize their potentialities as human beings. Too often we are apt to take the achievement of civilized life for granted, to assume that what is will always be. Yet the forces of barbarism are always present both in man and in society and constantly threaten to undo the work of centuries. We were all appalled when the forces of barbarism took over the reins of political power in Germany, a nation famous for its civilized achievements in the realms of philosophy, music and art. Civilization there appeared to be but a thin veneer, its achievements swept aside in a moment of bestial passion. What happened there can happen anywhere for the forces of barbarism are as universal as man's civilized achievements. Indeed man himself embodies both potentialities.

What we know as Western civilization has many roots and a long history. Its achievements have been established in numerous institutions and habitual ways of acting. Yet tradition alone cannot guarantee its continued existence unless each generation understands that tradition and appropriates it as its own. It is through teaching and learning that civilization is sustained and perpetuated. The great teachers are those who cherish the wisdom of the past and make it relevant to the present. Professor Yves Simon was such a teacher and his death in 1961 was a loss to education. The lectures reproduced in the pages which follow demonstrate not only his skill as a teacher but reveal a sensitive, disciplined mind inspired by love of the good.

In these lectures Professor Simon explores the meaning of one of the foundations of Western civilization, namely, the conviction that there is an objective and universal justice which transcends men's particular expressions of justice. This teaching has been called the "natural law" tradition and it is a conviction which gives substantial meaning to what civilized men throughout our history have called "the rule of law." It lies at the very root of what we call constitutional government. And it is a long tradition which extends from Sophocles' *Antigone* to the present day. It asserts that there are certain ways of behaving which are appropriate to man simply by virtue of the fact that he is a human being. It presupposes that it makes sense to speak of "human nature," that man has a nature as well as a history.

But it is not a tradition which has gone unchallenged and there are many today who find it untenable. It is sometimes asserted that if the natural law conviction were true we should expect all men everywhere to agree upon its content. Since we do not find this universal agreement there is no such thing as natural law or universal justice. Such critics point to the diversity of moral customs throughout the world as though this were a clinching argument. Such criticism is as old as the tradition itself and, though they are rarely identified by the same name, the Sophists are still with us and still repeating many of the same arguments. Yet what clamors for explanation is not the diversity of moral custom throughout the world but the universal fact that men everywhere under very different circumstances impose *some* restraints on conduct and defend some customs as more appropriate than others. And it is certainly more than subjective preference for our own standards of conduct that leads us to describe some moral customs as superior to others.

This is but one of the problems with which a student of the natural law tradition must be concerned, and it is characteristic of Professor Simon's mind and spirit that he does not avoid the difficult problems. The reader will be impressed not only with the honesty but with the philosophical skill with which Professor Simon examines the theoretical difficulties of his subject. He writes not as a polemicist but as a philosopher. He is less concerned with winning an argument than with exploring the truth of the matter. The tradition of natural law embraces a variety of philosophical doctrines and it has served different ideological purposes: serious study of natural law begins with dialectic and history. Moreover, an understanding of the nature of positive law, the "law of the land," is a logical prerequisite to the discussion of natural law. As Professor Simon points out, the truth of natural law is not affected by "the popular belief—shared by a great variety of philosophical thinkers—that a genuinely demonstrated proposition necessarily entails factual consensus, and that failure to cause consensus is perfect evidence of failure to attain demonstrativeness." Such a view "ignores the unpleasant fact that contingency affects intellectual life as certainly as it does the growth of plants in our forests and in our cultivated fields. There are departments of knowledge where demonstration, no matter how flawless, is unlikely to entail factual agreement except within small circles of kindred minds."

Professor Simon warns us against the tendency "to assume that natural law decides ... incomparably more issues than it is actually able to decide." Natural law is not some ready-made code waiting only for positive enactment for fulfillment but a guide to action. Professor Simon reminds us that many questions call for the exercise of prudence and we should not expect to settle moral questions with the certainty and assurance with which we solve a mathematical problem. He recognizes that the question "How do we know natural law?" is a difficult one to answer. But he helps us in seeking an answer by distinguishing between the "way of cognition" and the "way of inclination." In the concluding section of his book he gives some attention to the sense in which we can speak of progress in the knowledge of what is required by natural law. This knowledge is not something static nor is it "given all at once." Like every thing which is human it can grow in perfection. To explore the meaning of what today we call "social justice" in the light of the natural law tradition is the task to which he summons those of us who share his conviction that there is an objective and universal justice that does not derive from the opinions of men but sits in judgment of those opinions.

We owe a debt of gratitude to Professor Vukan Kuic, a former student of Professor Simon, for making these lectures available to all of us.

JOHN H. HALLOWELL
Professor of Political Science

Duke University
Durham, N. C.

Editor's Preface

THIS WORK has its origin in the course on "The Problem of Natural Law" given by the late Professor Yves R. Simon at the University of Chicago in the winter quarter of 1958. The lectures, including the class discussions, were recorded on tape, on his own initiative, by Mr. Richard Marco Blow, who also made the arrangements for the typescripts. The first nine lectures, corresponding here to chapters 1-4, were revised by Professor Simon in a separate manuscript; the remaining seven lectures, chapters 5-6, were partially edited by Professor Simon on the original typescript. All this material was made available to me in the fall of 1961.

It has been my good fortune to have been a student of Professor Simon from 1954 to 1956—and ever since that time, when I, myself, began teaching. In editing this essay, I have followed a simple though not necessarily an easy rule: not to be bound by words on paper, but also not to take away and not to add anything. The only relevant exception are the Notes in which my intention was to provide samples from and ready references to primary sources and a guide to Professor Simon's other works. For both the text and the notes I assume the proper responsibility of an editor.

I am deeply grateful to Mrs. Yves R. Simon both for the honor of this editorship and for her continuous help in all the stages of my work. The Research Committee of the University of Alabama supported the project with a grant in the summer of 1962. Professor Frank O'Malley of the University of Notre Dame and Professor Iredell Jenkins of the University of Alabama read the entire manuscript. Professors John Glanville of the Graduate School, St. John's University, Clifford G. Kossel, S. J., of the Mount Saint Michael's Seminary, Joseph Evans, Director of the Jacques Maritain Center at the University of Notre Dame, and J. B. McMinn of the University of Alabama, responded readily with advice on special points. Through his understanding and cooperation, Edwin A. Quain, S. J., Director of the Fordham University Press, made the preparation of the manuscript for publication pleasant and easy. I acknowledge the services of all with gratitude. And, if an editor may do so, I would like, with Mrs. Simon's full concurrence, to dedicate this book to other students of Yves R. Simon, past and future.

Introduction

YVES SIMON OBSERVES IN *The Tradition of Natural Law* that "There would be no eternal return of natural law without an everlasting opposition to natural law. . . . [T]his opposition thrives on the contrast between the notion of actions that are right or wrong by nature, and the lack of uniformity which we observe in actual judgments" (4).

The contrast between natural and universal laws and the manifest diversity and imperfection of human institutions is a contrast as persistent as any in the history of Western philosophy. Simon contends that the contrast between nature and convention is implicit in three irrepressible questions that attend our ordinary experience in matters of law: Is a positive law just or unjust? Upon what grounds is positive law to be changed? And should a manifestly wicked law be obeyed? (112–16).[1]

If we take historical experience as our guide, it is difficult to imagine a legal or political culture in which such questions would never arise or be taken seriously. Wherever there exists war, or the maldistribution of economic resources, or political despotism, or disputes that attend the litigation of rights—in short, wherever a serious imperfection is perceived in human practices and institutions—the questions leading to natural law will emerge. At least in Western culture, not only has discussion of natural law arisen more or less spontaneously under the pressures of practical problems; it has also become ingrained in the practical discourse and theoretical repertoire of our legal, political, and ecclesiastical institutions. The contrast between nature and convention, which sustains the theme of natural law, can be found in the declarations of international legal bodies, in constitutions and in bills of rights, in the legal briefs of revolutions, and in the seminal texts of legal and political theory which are used in universities and professional schools. Hence, natural law is not merely an idea, but a theory that is taught and learned within legal institutions.

The lectures which *The Tradition of Natural Law* comprises were delivered at the University of Chicago in 1958. Since that time, the issue of natural law continues to be enthusiastically asserted and debated. In the English-speaking world, for example, Lon Fuller's *The Morality of Law* (1964) and John Finnis' *Natural Law and Natural Rights* (1980) represent important scholarly contributions to the subject. Despite the decline of neo-scholasticism, there is as much, if not more, being written about natural law today than during the time of Simon's career.[2]

In the practical realm of law and politics we see natural law asserted and debated on all fronts. For example, in the struggle for civil rights, Martin Luther King's well-known essay, "Letter from a Birmingham Jail" appealed to the natural law to justify civil disobedience.[3] In American constitutional law, natural law theory has also become a prominent subject of debate with such issues as racial justice, privacy, abortion, and, above all, the problem of judicial review. Should a judiciary use natural principles of justice in interpreting the positive law? One nominee to the Supreme Court was rejected (Robert Bork, 1987), while another was nearly rejected (Clarence Thomas, 1991), among other reasons, because of their respective views on natural law. Curiously, Judge Bork was criticized for dismissing the idea of judicial uses of natural law, while Judge Thomas was criticized for being too enamored of the concept. And in what surely testifies to the international appeal of the notion of natural rights, no sooner had the Marxist regime fallen in the Soviet Union than the Soviet Congress of People's Deputies adopted a "Declaration of Human Rights and Freedoms," the first article of which states: "Every person possesses natural, inalienable and inviolable rights and freedoms."[4]

Simon was entirely correct about the "eternal return" of natural law theory. The notion speaks for itself—rooted in the experiential soil of the contrast between law as it is and law as it ought to be. Nevertheless, there are more or less persuasive criticisms of natural law which run the gamut from nihilistic denials of objective moral truth to more sophisticated and expert questions about the very meaning of a "law" of nature. Of the latter and more serious sort, one criticism is especially prominent and potent in modern philosophy. Since the sixteenth century it has been proposed—in optics, physics, and other natural sciences—that law can be predicated of nature only insofar as events are necessary in the physical order, and that this necessity is a function of predictability.[5] How, for the purposes of humane issues related to practical reason, philosophers asked, can law be predicated of nature without falling into an equivocation regarding the meaning of natural law? Does natural law denote what is necessary and predictable about physical events, or does it denote moral injunctions governing human choice? This dilemma underlies the philosophical, in contrast with the merely logical, problem of how to interrelate fact and value, description and prescription, and the causal principles of necessity and freedom in moral science. Although it is by no means the only basis for the cluster of ideas that present themselves under the name of "legal positivism," the effort to avoid an equivocal meaning of law is certainly one of the concerns that inspires the positivist challenge to the tradition of natural law.

While the success of the modern sciences does not remove the contrast between nature and convention, it certainly makes it difficult to align either moral or legal norms on the side of nature. In modern times, philosophical perplexity over how to maintain the contrast between nature and convention has led natural law theorists in two directions. On the one hand, natural law can be conceived along physicalist lines, to denote those psycho-physiological necessities which uniformly attend and influence any legal or moral culture. Thomas Hobbes, David Hume, and, more recently, H. L. A. Hart have keyed the *humane* meaning of natural law to pervasive human necessities, principally those connected to survival.[6] The fundamental contrast between nature and convention is thought to be useful insofar as the conditions of survival are predictable, rooted in nature, and cannot be said to depend upon the merely subjective or idiosyncratic views of either individuals or cultures. Whatever merits there are to this position, it retains the moral meaning of natural law only in the weakest sense—as a kind of background consideration for any scheme of positive law.

Another tradition, typified by Kant's dictum that one "[m]ust act as if the maxim of your action were to become through your will a universal law of nature," emphasizes the noumenal goods of freedom.[7] As developed by many modern theorists, autonomy is a concept that embraces both a moral norm and a natural fact. Given the self-determinative capacity of freedom, human agents must be regarded as ends in themselves. This view undergirds a scheme of rights and duties which set norms for positive law. Whereas the modern physicalist tradition focuses upon certain empirically evident needs of survival, the tradition stemming from Kant stresses such spiritual and moral goods as self-constitution, respect, and personal autonomy. Despite the popularity of Kantian-like formulations of the tradition of natural law, it remains unclear why the moral law enjoining respect for persons should be called "natural" law.[8] Is natural law something given antecedent to choice, or is natural law an ideal constructed by human practical reason? In any case, both the physicalist and the autonomist bear witness to the fact that philosophers are not willing to dispense altogether with the rhetoric of natural law.

II

Given the practical and institutional incentives for maintaining *some* theory of natural law, however tenuous even in the face of philosophical challenges to the concept, Simon adopts what may seem to the reader a very cautious approach to the subject. In *The Tradition of Natural Law* he sets out "to see the difficulties where they are and to puncture a few myths" (13). The reader will not find in these pages a systematic exposition and defense of natural law—once again, the persistence of both the question and the need for natural law speaks for itself—rather, Simon invites the reader to take a dialectical and historical approach to the *problems* that attend natural law theory.

Of course, there can be no doubt that Simon embraced what, from a philosophical position, would be called a premodern view of natural law. His understanding of the interrelation of epistemological, ontological, and metaphysical elements of natural law theory is, on the whole, Thomistic.[9] The natural law, first grasped in the actions and goods connatural to our inclinations, bespeaks finality in nature, and ultimately a divine creator. Simon has little use for theories of natural law which sidestep the problem of natural teleology or the theological terms of the issue. But the fact remains that *The Tradition of Natural Law* is meant to address not the critics of natural law, but the problems and myths that have beset its proponents.

The chief virtue of this work is Simon's effort to undertake a clear and honest reckoning of the problems that have to be settled if there is to be anything other than a superficial, if not ideological, revival of the tradition of natural law. Although some of Simon's remarks reflect concerns of the immediate post–World War II period, his general line of questioning about the tradition of natural law is still current and valid. This volume remains a discerningly reasoned and handy introduction to the problems of natural law.

It might prove useful to the reader to outline in brief some of the problems and myths Simon addresses. We will turn, first, to the problems which Simon treats under the general headings of history and doctrine. Then, we will take up what is perhaps the most penetrating discussion in the volume: namely, Simon's analysis of the problems of consensus and ideology. As we will see, Simon believes that the greatest danger to the tradition of natural law is not its cultured critics, but rather the tendency of its allies to reduce natural law to an ideology in order to form a political or legal consensus about objective values.

Simon sets forth the first problem at the outset of this volume. He writes: "The subject with which we are concerned is difficult because it is engaged in an overwhelming diversity of doctrinal contexts and of historical accidents. It is doubtful that this double diversity, doctrinal and historical, can so be mastered as to make possible a completely orderly exposition of the subject of natural law" (5). Historically, there is not really *a* tradition of natural law, but several traditions. The fundamental contrast between nature and convention is open to quite diverse formulations, and this diversity seems to depend in large measure upon sociological, political, and other institutional contexts.

In the work of Aquinas, for example, "nature" is not simply a term of contrast with human positive law, but it is also something to be seen in contrast with other modes of divine governance. Accordingly, the natural law, which is God's way of governing via secondary causality, is distinguished from divine positive law given in the Decalogue, as well as from the grace given in the *lex nova*. Whereas Aquinas' interests concerned a theological scheme of laws and jurisdictions, modern theorists, as Simon explains, appealed "to nature against constituted authority" (8). During the revolutionary era, the contrast between natural and civil society served the vindication of natural rights of individuals against the alleged historical and divine rights of the prince (36). During the nineteenth century, the notion of a "natural order" was deployed by economic theorists in order to sharpen a contrast with political economies which are "planned out" (37). In their view, "nature" has little to do with any cosmological or theological order; rather, it concerns the principles embedded in human (economic) activities which need to be protected, no doubt in the form of natural rights, against governmental artifice and tampering. In this respect, Simon is impressed by how difficult it is to extract the doctrinal from the historical. The reader will note that in his concluding chapter Simon contends that a philosophical reconsideration of natural law cannot be undertaken without a "keen awareness" of the historical sources (159). In particular, he urges further historical study of the modern identification of "nature" not with law, but with the claim to rights (120, 160).

A second problem Simon considers throughout the volume is how to take a properly philosophical view of natural law. Simon contends that it is "vain and unprofitable" to argue about natural law without attending to its various theoretical presuppositions (160). Natural law, he observes, is a "subject of direct, intense, daily, and tragic interest to all sorts of people whose philosophic tools may well be primitive" (14). Whatever the reasons that lead lawyers, politicians, or revolutionaries to *use* a theory of natural law, the philosophical questions attendant to natural law stubbornly resist reduction to the resolution of practical needs. Natural law, Simon writes,

is related in the most inescapable way to profound issues of theoretical philosophy. Thus, the difficulties proper to philosophy are inescapably present in any discussion involving natural law. From this it follows that whenever there is a good reason to avoid these difficulties, there will also be a good reason to leave natural law out of the picture, whether by denying that it exists or by acting as if its existence did not matter [63].

Particularly in Chapter 3, "Some Theoretical Questions," and in Chapter 5, "Natural Law," Simon tries at least to clarify some of the main philosophical problems of natural law. These include (*a*) the differences between pre-modern and modern understandings of the term "nature," especially with regard to the problem of finality in nature (44–53); (*b*) the problem of necessity and freedom (57–60, 122–23); (*c*) the problem of whether a theory of natural law must presuppose the idea of nature as divinely legislated (62, 139); and (*d*) the problem of the relation between reason and nature (137). Simon is dubious that the modern philosophies of nature since Descartes have adequate theoretical resources to maintain a tradition of natural law that can resist submersion into ideology. *The Tradition of Natural Law* gives little comfort to those who would want to revive natural law theory without an adequate theoretical foundation.

Although Simon insists that it is "vain and unprofitable" to argue about natural law without addressing its philosophical problems, even here he is wary about the best way to proceed. In the conclusion, for instance, he admits that it is not entirely clear whether the issues built into natural law theory ought to be posited systematically according to their natural order, or whether the subject calls for a dialectical treatment in which the logical, ontological, and metaphysical problems are addressed at the point where they might arise (160).[10] How far can one get into the issue of natural law without raising the problem of nature and finality in nature? How far can one proceed until the issue of God comes to the fore? On the one hand, Simon wants us to exercise a due suspicion of natural law theories that evade problems of "theoretic philosophy." On the other, he is reluctant to settle the problem of method decisively. Natural law, after all, does not first arise as a theoretical exercise. Moreover, as Simon himself never tired of reminding his readers, there may be kinds of practical certitude which are never entirely communicable in the form of theory and demonstration (133).[11] As we will note later, Simon argues that the root and nerve of natural law—the source that makes theories about it possible—is reached not by a philosophical mode of cognition, but by a connatural grasp of the good via inclination.

For Simon, there is nothing contradictory in holding that natural law is inescapably theoretical and properly philosophical, and that our grasp of natural law runs ahead of our often clumsy efforts to formulate it in cogent philosophical terms. He does not wish to slacken the tension between the pre-theoretical and -philosopical dimensions of the issue, among other reasons because he correctly saw that unless this tension is maintained there is no way to extricate the tradition of natural law from the problems of rationalism and ideology. Simon argued elsewhere that "a purely rational moral philosophy is essentially misleading."[12] He held this position not only because of his emphasis upon the virtues and the importance of affective order in human agency, but also because of his estimation of the importance of theological issues—both in terms of the problem of sin (the discrepancy between *de jure* and *de facto* possibilities of making sense of natural law), and in terms of the problem of revelation (the subordination of natural law theory to what faith knows about the final end).[13] The zone of natural law amenable to philosophical explication is limited, as it were, from below and from above.

III

Above all, Simon calls attention to the problem of ideology in contemporary efforts to reassert or reclaim the tradition of natural law:

Our time has witnessed a new birth of belief in natural law concomitantly with the success of existentialism, which represents the most thorough criticism of natural law ever voiced by philosophers. Against such powers of destruction we feel the need for an ideology of natural law. The current interest in this subject certainly expresses an aspiration of our society at a time when the foundations of common life and of just relations are subjected to radical threats. No matter how sound these aspirations may be, they are quite likely to distort philosophic treatments. For a number of years we have been witnessing a tendency, in teachers and preachers, to assume that natural law decides, with the universality proper to the necessity of essences, incomparably more issues than it is actually able to decide. There is a tendency to treat in terms of natural law questions which call for treatment in terms of prudence. It should be clear that any concession to this tendency is bound promptly to cause disappointment and skepticism [23].

There are a number of thoughts in this passage that we should at least briefly touch upon.

By "ideology" Simon means a "system of propositions" that refer not so much to any real state of affairs as to the "aspirations" of a society at a certain time (16–17). It is to be distinguished from philosophy because it reduces truth to a utilitarian function, and because it drapes contingent social–historical aspirations in the mantle of universal truths. Simon gives as example the nineteenth-century southern case of slavery. As the controversy escalated, what began as a legal accommodation of slavery on pragmatic grounds became a "universal law." What was once acknowledged to be solely the creature of positive law, became in the opinion of Justice Taney, in *Dred Scott v. Sandford* (1857), the most natural and inflexible of rights. History is replete with such examples, where one or another expression of natural law is used to fend off what one class perceives to be threats to its interests. Simon makes it clear, however, that abuse of natural law does not occur only in those cases where natural law is used in defense of a morally illegitimate or despotic order. It occurs as well in situations where, for otherwise worthy purposes, the theory is used by revolutionaries, reformers, and clergy to bring about justice or to respond to moral relativism. Indeed, in our time and culture, natural law is invoked as a response to the breakdown of tradition, to moral relativism and nihilism, to various species of utilitarianism, and to legal positivism. It is expected to be an all-purpose antidote to the estrangements of modernity. Called upon to remediate more than reasonably can be expected, natural law is liable to descend to ideology.

In taking stock of this problem, Simon concedes that a "philosophy unaffected by any ideological feature would involve a degree of perfection that human affairs do not admit of" (22). A "pure" philosophy in this regard is "almost impossible." In the first place, no philosopher, Simon notes, is ever able to escape fully the ideological influences of his society (25). In the second place, the very problems that make natural law intelligible are also the ones responsible for ideology. A pure philosophy that is either untainted by ideology, or in the service of no particular community, would require methods so extreme that we would have good reason to judge the methods themselves ideological. The problem of natural law, for Simon, must be located somewhere between the pressure of social aspirations and the ideal of a completely detached objectivity. There is no *a priori* way to say precisely how to take the measure of that in-between.

A society that perceives itself to have only the weapon of natural law theory to address the enemies of right reason is, no doubt, a society that will have trouble taking that measure. In *Practical Knowledge*, Simon contends that one of the reasons for the immoderate expectation with respect to any kind of moral theory is the "breakdown of tradition."[14] Once again, it needs to be said that without imperfections in traditions and customs, there would be no felt need to advert to natural law. Furthermore, the lack of adequate theoretical articulation of commonly held convictions can be one such imperfection. But what Simon has in mind is the breakdown of the pre-theoretical bases for moral consensus—bases that owe more to affective sources of order and common striving than to philosophy. We might speculate that certain features of modern society make natural law theory more rather than less necessary for the achievement of consensus about the *ordo juris*; and perhaps this explains, in part, why theories of natural law have proliferated in modernity, despite the fact that there remain only the thinnest philosophical and theological grounds to support them.

Whatever is the case in this regard, in *The Tradition of Natural Law* Simon makes the startling proposal that "when the theory of natural law seems to be commonly accepted and works as a factor of agreement, there are good reasons to suspect that it is embodied in an *ideology*" (66). This observation is apt to startle the American reader. For *his* tradition of natural law is part and parcel of the consensus about those "self-evident" truths voiced by Jefferson and Lincoln. Arguably, the American political and legal order was uniquely founded, and indeed re-founded, upon precisely that consensus expressed in the form of natural law propositions. What, then, does Simon mean when he says that we ought to suspect any consensus in which agreement about natural law plays a noticeable part? Might it not be a contradiction in terms to suggest that agreement about natural law constitutes *prima facie* grounds for suspecting the presence of ideology?

Any adequate answer to this question would take us into the details of Simon's theory of practical knowledge. It must suffice here to make a few remarks that will only skim the surface of the issue. Recall Simon's admonition that we be concerned about (*a*) our tendency to assume that natural law decides, with the universality proper to the necessity of essences, incomparably more issues than it is actually able to decide, and (*b*) our tendency to treat in terms of natural law questions that call for treatment in terms of prudence. Regarding natural law and the problem of consensus, Simon contends that there are limits to the kind of unanimity that can be achieved not only by law, but also by theory about practical matters.

"[L]aw," he says, "is a premise rather than a conclusion" (85). To the extent that the premises represent what is universal and necessary, the more they bespeak the character of law.[15] "Law is more at home in the realm of necessity. If any law is so grounded in a necessary state of affairs as to be unqualifiedly immutable, this is a law in the most excellent sense of the term" (84). Human legislative systems, however, participate unequally in the character of law, he notes, for the intermediate premises which generate determinate laws are usually premises connected to contingent conditions (86, 151). By contingent, Simon does not mean unintelligible; rather, he means that the rationality of the system of laws is not apodictic. Natural laws "have more the character of premises than positive laws [because] they are prior premises" (129). Though they may engender a kind of certitude, such axiomatic premises of natural law are not always clear either in the psychological sense (77) or in the sense of what can be communicated by demonstration (133).[16] It is very difficult, if not impossible, for the purpose of philosophical consensus to reduce analytically the plethora of premises embedded in a legislative system to those first axiomatic premises of natural law, and then, by dint of deductive exposition, to spin the laws back out according to irrefragable connectives.

While Simon does not reject the possibility of a reflective approach to first principles—from time to time a legal culture will find itself having to do so—he is wary about how much can be gained for the purpose of consensus. He points out, for example, that although we might expect unanimity about such notions as the subordination of the private to the common good (91), the keeping of contracts (133), and that at least some acts are wrong by their very essence (146), it is difficult to extract completely the premises from contingent conditions, but even more difficult to achieve unanimity about what the premises mean and how they ought to be formulated and applied in concrete cases.

Simon urges us to distinguish clearly between natural law and the function of positive law. The "formulas of positive law," he says, "are designed to hold men together, organize their cooperation, bring about uniformity in the behavior of indefinitely many individuals." Hence, it is "highly desirable that these formulas should command the assent of all persons concerned or most of them" (65). Positive law, in both its legislative and its adjudicative function, is appropriately directed to consensus. The positive lawyer seeks factual communicability as well as explanations of the law suited to widespread agreement. Moreover, in societies deeply divided on philosophical, social, and religious issues, the positive lawyer must compromise by formulating laws and explanations in a way that prescinds, as far as possible, from the terms of dissensus over deeper issues that divide the community.

The point to be made is that we must be careful not to seek in natural law exactly the same requirements and norms which are central to a system of positive laws. In short, it is a mistake to envisage natural law as a ready-made body of law (a meta-level positive law, as it were) to which the problems of human positive law can immediately be referred. When the function of positive law is extended to the issue of natural law, what happens is that the formulations of natural law are cut and trimmed to produce consensus. Accordingly, the necessary and universal premises of the law of nature bespeak the *ad hoc* political compromises of the moment. This is a recipe not only for skepticism, but for ideology.

In an important discussion in *The Tradition of Natural Law*, Simon also points out a peculiarity of law that it works against the grain of the ordinary life of practical reason. For practical reason is inexorably drawn not to essences or premises but to concrete judgment. In matters of practical reason, Simon emphasizes the difference between legislative reason, which issues the premises for action, and practical reason in the strict sense of the term, which regards action as the conclusion of its discourse. The "conclusion of the practical discourse implies, in the most essential fashion, a trait opposed to the rational character of law": namely, right reason in the singular and contingent matter of action (83). The function of law as a premise and the fully practical judgments of action are not reducible to one another. A traffic code, for example, sets certain injunctions as to how vehicles are to be operated. However, if such a code is to bring about uniformity of action, it cannot regulate every singular action, in every contingent circumstance. Good law is under the imperative to achieve adequate generality, and it is precisely this virtue of legislative reason that can prove to be a vice if it is confused with the operation of practical reasoning, in which generalities are never adequate to concrete judgments. Clearly, the positive law is no substitute for the myriad of intelligent judgments that have to be made on the part of drivers. On the other hand, if there is to be any common order in this regard, individual judgments and actions must be brought under general rules. "The principle of government by law," Simon notes, "is subject to such precarious conditions that, if it were not constantly reasserted, it soon would be destroyed by the opposite and complementary principle, viz., that of adequacy to contingent, changing, and unique circumstances" (84). The facts, explanations, and methods that concern legislative reason overlap with, but do not entirely constitute, the ultimate act of practical reason.

Simon insists that this presents real limits to the role of law in achieving consensus about practical matters. Between law as a set of premises, and fully determinate action, there is "always a space" to be filled by something that cannot be fully expressed in the form of written law or, for that matter, in any abstract formulation. Therefore, Simon stresses the importance of rectitude of the appetite—the virtues—in reaching unanimity about action (156). As he says in *Practical Knowledge*, "The practical judgment, in order to be true and certain, ought to proceed not by logical connection with axioms (such a connection is impossible in contingent matters), but by way of virtuous inclination. This judgment is an act of knowledge through affective connaturality."[17] In a similar vein, in *A General Theory of Authority*, he contends that "[s]ince unanimity cannot be established in these practical matters by the power of demonstration, the ideally clever and virtuous members of a community cannot be unanimous in more than fortuitous fashion unless a determined course of action is demanded by the virtuous inclination of their hearts."[18]

What, then, is the role of natural law in achieving practical unanimity? Simon remarks that the problem of how we know the natural law "is not an easy one to answer or even to approach" (126). One of the reasons for this difficulty is that natural law "is known by way of inclination before it is known by way of cognition" (132). As Aquinas says, the inclinations are the "seeds" (*seminalia*) both of the common principles of law and of the virtues.[19] Both the order of precepts and the order of virtue stem from the order of inclinations. These inclinations are the first way we recognize both the objectives of action (the good of life, friendship, etc.) and, in a very rudimentary manner, the actions that are congruent with those objectives. Accordingly, the goods as end(s) and the goods as action(s) are seminally contained in knowledge *per inclinationem*. But these inclinations are not sufficient for either a body of law or fully practical judgments about action. As premises given to cognition via the inclinations, they need to be spelled out in the form of conclusions, applied to individual cases, and eventually organized into a coherent scheme of positive laws. Simon points out that considerable time can elapse between what is grasped by affective connaturality and what is understood in the way of explanatory reasons (158).[20] Whether for the purposes of a legislative system or for the purposes of the personal and intersubjective dimension of practical reasoning, much is required—the tutoring of inclinations by a tradition, and the acquisition of the habits of volitional rectitude—in order to achieve some measure of understanding and unanimity about what is enjoined on us by nature.

On this view, the natural law admits of two distinct though interrelated meanings that are apt to be confused because of their original unity in what is first grasped by inclination: (*a*) natural law can designate the premises for action, which can be formulated in preceptive or legal-like terms; (*b*) natural law can designate the dispositional elements constituting rectitude of action, which consists principally in the affective habits. In other words, natural law embraces both the issue of law and the issue of virtue. Because the inchoate knowledge of both is first given in the inclinations, it is a tricky problem how to distinguish and emphasize properly one or the other of these themes in a theory of natural law. Whereas modern natural law theories have tended to emphasize the legal and rationally determinable side of the problem of natural law, Simon emphasizes the affective side. If the knowledge of natural law is first enjoyed *per inclinationem*, then it would seem that Simon has the more correct point of view. In any case, his position on the role of the inclinations explains his reluctance throughout this volume to deliver natural law into the hands of a pure practical reason, which seeks to bring about a fully rationalized ground for moral or legal consensus about action.

In summary, Simon's caution about the role of natural law theory in creating consensus is due to his understanding of the following issues. *First*, the difference between the premises of law and the conclusions of prudence is irreducible; and what is communicable about the former is not necessarily so of the latter. *Second*, the premises of law which are subject to controversy are not easily, or even advisably, extractable from their contingent and circumstantial conditions. *Third*, there are important differences between what can be expected of human positive law, of theories about natural law, and of affective communion in bringing about common assent to the terms of action. *Fourth*, the premises grasped through inclination are only the beginning of the legal and affective themes of natural law. For the purposes of either law or virtue, agreement about the natural law is hard won, requiring considerable time and experience.

Whatever the difficulties in theorizing about the natural law, *The Tradition of Natural Law* does not iron them out in any way that kills the sense of mystery about the subject. "One of the social functions of philosophers," Simon writes, "when they speak of natural law, is to remind men that their own nature, the moral nature, the universe of morality, is no less mysterious than this physical universe" (40).

RUSSELL HITTINGER

The Catholic University of America
Washington, D.C.

NOTES

1. For a discussion of the way the problem of natural law is disclosed in the contrast between nature and custom, see Robert Sokolowski, "Knowing Natural Law," in *Pictures, Quotations, and Distinctions* (Notre Dame: University of Notre Dame Press, 1992), chap. 14.

2. For a sense of how many different kinds of issues are discussed today under the rubric of "natural law," see *Natural Law Theory*, ed. Robert P. George (Oxford: Clarendon, 1992). For a survey of some of its contemporary uses in legal theory, see Russell Hittinger, "Liberalism and the American Natural Law Tradition," *Wake Forest Law Review*, 25 (1990), 429–99. Finally, for a compendium of primary texts and bibliographical material on classical modern natural law theories, see J. B. Schneewind, *Moral Philosophy From Montaigne to Kant* I (Cambridge: Cambridge University Press, 1990), 67–198.

3. In *Why We Can't Wait* (New York: Harper & Row, 1963), pp. 77–100.

4. *The New York Times*, Saturday, September 7, 1991, A-5.

5. Jane E. Ruby, "The Origins of Scientific 'Law,' " *Journal of the History of Ideas*, 47 (1986), 341–59.

6. For the clearest contemporary formulation of this position, see H. L. A. Hart, "The Minimum Content of Natural Law," *The Concept of Law* (Oxford: Clarendon, 1961), pp. 189–95.

7. Immanuel Kant, *Grounding for the Metaphysics of Morals*, trans. James W. Ellington (Indianapolis: Hackett, 1981), #421, 30.

8. For a useful survey of deontological approaches to natural law, see Lloyd

L. Weinreb, "Natural Law Without Nature," *Natural Law and Justice* (Cambridge: Harvard University Press, 1987), chap. 4.

9. For example, Chapter 4 ("The Definition of Law") is basically a reflection on the first question in Aquinas' treatise on law in the *Summa theologiae* (I–II, q. 90).

10. The reader will find it illuminating to compare Simon with two of his contemporary Catholic natural law theorists, Jacques Maritain and John Courtney Murray. In *Man and the State* (Chicago: The University of Chicago Press, 1951), Maritain took a more benign view of what could be accomplished by way of common agreements about natural law despite dissensus over the explanatory principles. Regarding human rights, Maritain endorsed what he called a "basic *practical* ideology" and a secular "faith" on natural rights. While there are many areas of agreement between Maritain and Simon, the reader will note that Simon was more cautious about the ideological factor. John Courtney Murray, on the other hand, stressed far more than Simon did the resources (especially in America) for theoretical agreement. In Chapter 13 of *We Hold These Truths* (New York: Doubleday, 1964), Murray argued that even the metaphysical premises of natural law are amenable to the contemporary mind. Once again, Simon took a more cautious approach.

11. On the incommunicability of the ultimate practical judgment, see Simon's *Practical Knowledge*, ed. Robert J. Mulvaney (New York: Fordham University Press, 1991), p. 24.

12. Ibid., p. 95.

13. Ibid., pp. 90–96, 151–52.

14. Ibid., p. 97. Here, Simon speculates the hyper-need to achieve consensus about action through rational explanation is due to the breakdown of tradition.

15. See his discussion of necessity and contingency in law in *A General Theory of Authority* (Notre Dame: University of Notre Dame Press, 1962; repr. 1991), p. 20.

16. Aquinas, for example, was careful in speaking of the *per se nota* status of the first premises of natural law to distinguish between what is *per se notum* in itself (*secundum se*) and what is *per se notum* to us (*quo ad nos*). *Quo ad nos*, a self-evident proposition could require considerable learning before it is grasped (*Summa theologiae* I, 2, 1; I–II, 94, 2).

17. *Practical Knowledge*, p. 20.

18. *General Theory of Authority*, p. 33. For his discussion of the differences between the respective functions of law and authority, see pp. 20, 48.

19. *Summa theologiae* I–II, 51, 1.

20. *Practical Knowledge*, p. 34.

PART ONE

The Problem / 1

THE THEORY OF natural law, attacked and rejected many times, always comes back with fresh energy. This is well said by the title of Professor Heinrich Rommen's book, *Die ewige Wiederkehr des Naturrechts* (The Eternal Return of Natural Law).[1] Today natural law once again arouses keen and general interest but it is also more thoroughly negated than it ever was. Legal positivism is a very old thing; it was familiar to Aristotle. In our time, however, positivism is supplemented by existentialism, a philosophy dedicated to the proposition that man has no nature but only history.

True, we all act as if there were a natural law, just as we all act as if there were such a thing as natural finality. But when we begin to talk about finality in nature there is always somebody to voice the belief that modern science has ruled out this concept forever. Likewise, in discussions about natural law our words are often at variance with our spontaneous beliefs. The most common objection, which is also psychologically the most powerful, can be summed up as follows: if there were a natural law, there would be more uniformity in ideas about the right and the wrong, and in the customs and

3

institutions which embody these ideas. It is a very simple reasoning in the well known form: $[(p \to q) . \sim q] \to \sim p$. If there is such a thing as natural law (p), a certain uniformity follows (q); but in our experience we do not find such uniformity $(\sim q)$, and we infer that there is no such thing as natural law $(\sim p)$. But is it true that if there were a natural law, there should be more uniformity than we actually find in opinions, in philosophies, in customs, in institutions, and especially in the judgments about the right and the wrong embodied in customs and institutions? Is it true that the reality of natural law would entail uniformities that, in fact, we do not observe?

Suppose we discuss a particular problem of natural law. We are friendly; we have much in common. And yet, if we discuss such a subject as, say, assassination, we may not agree completely. We certainly all hold that, other things being equal, it is better not to cut the throat of a twelve-year-old child than to cut it. Our agreement would certainly persist if it were a question of murdering a child of seven, a child of three, a newly-born baby. If the baby is not yet born, agreement is less certain, and if we speak of an embryo of only a few weeks, we may well become sharply divided. But if we assume that murdering children is either right or wrong by nature, should we not expect to find a more permanent unity in our opinions? Does the absence of q destroy p? It does if, and only if, p implies q.

There would be no eternal return of natural law without an everlasting opposition to natural law. Again, this opposition thrives on the contrast between the notion of actions that are right or wrong by nature, and the lack of uniformity which we observe in actual judgments. If the right or wrong of murdering unborn babies is decided by nature, why should we not be completely agreed on such an important subject? Even in a well-defined social group divergencies are not inconceivable; in the world at large sharp clashes of opinion are certain to occur. There is a rumor that modern ethnology has demonstrated the absence of uniformity among peoples in matters of so-called natural law. That is rather naïve. This lack of uniformity was well known long, long before what is called modern science came to exist. In fact, modern ethnologists would be rather more critical and skeptical about stories of strange customs than men of antiquity or of the Renaissance. These were eager to believe travellers' stories, which are just as reliable as fishermen's stories. When we hear strange tales about a remote land, we want proof; but for the men of the Renaissance it sometimes seems that no story was too wild to be true. And the texts of Aristotle (*Ethics* 5.7.1134b; *Rhetoric* 1.13.1373b.) to which we have alluded suffice to make us aware that in his time also there were travellers' stories about the mores of other nations. Between Persia and Greece cultural differences were known to be great. And some thinkers even then proclaimed that these differences demonstrated that there was no such thing as natural law. The opposition to it is as old as the theory.[2]

Let us try to explain, no matter how briefly, why the subject of natural law is so difficult. There is no easy subject in philosophy, but there are circumstances which make a subject particularly hard to organize and expound. The subject with which we are concerned is difficult because it is engaged in an overwhelming diversity of doctrinal contexts and of historical accidents. It is doubtful that this double diversity, doctrinal and historical, can so be mastered as to make possible a completely orderly exposition of the subject of natural law.

DOCTRINAL CONNECTIONS

More or less explicitly, every practical doctrine presupposes some theoretical positions. The theoretical issues whose treatment is logically presupposed by the philosophy of natural law are formidable. To take only the most obvious of them, what do we have to say about the unity of human nature? Under the Nazis it was held that there is a greater distance between the highest and the lowest races of men than between the lowest races of men and the highest races of animals. Strikingly, this proposition is already mentioned by Rousseau in his *Discourse on the Origin of Inequality*.[3] He does not give any reference and all one can say is that such a proposition fits nicely the pattern of sensationism and materialism prevalent about the middle of the eighteenth century. To be sure, in a consistently sensationist philosophy the difference between man and other animals is only one of degree. But this consequence of sensationism, which might have produced Nazis, or cannibals, in the enlightened society of the eighteenth century, was held in check by a contrary current in ethical sentiment. Those things sometimes happen: at a certain time a theoretical philosophy which inclines minds and souls in a certain direction may be held in check by the predominance of an opposite sentiment. The golden age of sensationism was also the golden age of the rights of man and of universalistic ethics.

Whether there is such a thing as a universal human nature is a question which cannot be dodged; it is a question that must be settled before proceeding to the discussion of natural law. But what do we mean by "universal"? Here is a difficulty which has always vexed logicians and philosophers: the problem of the universal. When we say "man," or "dog," what do we mean? Do we designate a nature possessed of unity outside the mind, a Platonic archetype? Or do we use a word and a concept to which nothing corresponds in the real world except a collection of individuals? This is a problem whose examination began, at the very latest, with Socrates, and will go on so long as philosophic intelligence is at work. But, clearly, if natural law means anything in a nominalistic philosophy, it must be something widely different from what it means in a philosophy of the Aristotelian type, according to which there exist universal natures although they do *not* enjoy, as in Plato, a state of *positive unity* outside the mind.[4]

Let us confess that it is meaningless to argue seriously about natural law without having ever raised the question of the universals. Men with legal training are not afraid to write for or against natural law; it would be interesting to see how certain, or uncertain, they are on the meaning of the universal, on the logic of the universal. A worse thing is that the pronouncements of logicians on this subject are often ambiguous. The word "class," as used in logic, means either of two things, and one generally does not know which is indicated. Class may designate a genus or a species, a universal whole whose parts are called subjective because the universal whole is sharply distinguished from other wholes by its ability to be predicated, in its whole meaning, of each of its "parts" or subjects. Class may also designate a set, a collection. Now, to say that Socrates is a man is correct, if by "man" we mean a universal whole, a whole which constitutes a paradoxical case of totality inasmuch as it can be identified with each and every one of its parts, taken one by one. As a universal it is potential, not a positive but only a negative or open unity that, in the act of predicating, is seen—without loss of meaning but, on the contrary, in realization of its meaning—to close with the actual, positive unity of each single subject. If by "man," on the contrary, we mean the set of all existent men, or the set of all men that have existed or are existent, or the set of all men that have existed or are existent or will exist —then, clearly, man no longer can be predicated of Socrates. One can say that Mr. Douglas is a member of the Senate, but one cannot say that he is the Senate, or that he is senate. A set cannot be predicated of any of its parts.[5] Thus when the word class is used without the specification either that it stands for "universal whole" or that it stands for "set," we may be following either one of two lines of reasoning which remain essentially different even when both chance to be valid. Perhaps some discussion on natural law can be had without this issue being decided. But philosophy begins when we come to understand that issues of this kind are worth examining and deciding.

HISTORICAL CONTEXTS

The problem of the universals supplies an example of the doctrinal contexts in which the subject of natural law is engaged. It is obvious that the theory of natural law is opposed by the nominalistic tendency and probably would be made impossible by a strictly and consistently nominalistic philosophy, if such could exist. Let us now see how historical situations may work for or against the theory of natural law.

Famous examples readily come to mind. Think of the late eighteenth century. The American and the French Revolutions were widely different historical and sociological processes, and yet in both cases appeal was made to nature against constituted authority. The appeal was to the natural order against a factual state of affairs; the energies of nature were expected to end detested accidents of history. In the American Revolution the purpose was to get rid of a government in which the Colonies were not represented. In the French Revolution the problem was much more radical: it was to get rid of an extremely complex political and social system which restrained the ambitions of the rising and already powerful bourgeoisie. But notice that the belligerent universalism of these two revolutions was not entirely consistent. This is evident from the fact that the American Constitution acknowledged slavery, albeit in reserved and apologetic terms; and a few years later the French revolutionary government declared that the principle of human equality did not apply to the colored people of the West Indies who were, for an influential part of the bourgeoisie, a convenient pool of cheap labor.

In the nineteenth century, it is interesting to observe in connection with the problem of nationalities how certain circumstances work against the theory of natural law and in favor of something which came to be called historical law. The question of the right of nationalities may be stated as follows: does a particular group characterized, say, by language, tradition, and culture, have a right to constitute a political unit of its own? Think of the Austro-Hungarian Empire. The Hungarian issue had been settled in 1848. The government of Franz-Joseph was a double monarchy, *die kaiserliche und königliche Regierung,* imperial for Austria and royal for Hungary. But the Empire comprised also Czechs, Slovaks, Slovenes and Croats, Rumanians, and Poles. These peoples claimed, in varying degrees of resolution and fierceness, that they had a right to constitute or join political entities coincident with national groups. The realization of these programs involved great difficulties. In order to satisfy Czech nationalism in 1918-1919, it was found necessary to construct a state made of Czechs, Slovaks, and German Bohemians, with a few Hungarians and a few Poles. This state was destroyed in 1938 when the German part of Bohemia was annexed to Germany. Insofar as the German Bohemians supported Hitlerian expansionism, it can be said that the same principle of nationalities which presided over the construction of the Czechoslovak state in 1918-1919, presided also over its destruction in 1938. The historical settlement of Bohemia was such that a Slavic state comprising Bohemia had to include an important German minority. The Munich agreement of 1938 did not deceive anybody; without the Sudetenland Czechoslovakia was impossible. After the second World War the situation was simplified by the expulsion of the German Bohemians.

In historical perspective the dangers involved in the satisfaction of national aspirations appear obvious. The principle of national self-determination—in the example just given—had destroyed an established state without guaranteeing peace under the new arrangement. But already in the nineteenth century a *historical right* theory was invoked against the natural right theory of the nation. According to this view, a political entity by the very fact of its historic existence, by the very fact that it had withstood and conquered historical difficulties over a long period of time, has a right to endure, even though some of its national components might like to secede. True, the historical right theory has also been used to satisfy national aspirations. But the point is precisely that at the turn of the century it was rather commonly held that the theory of natural law was a purely negative and destructive influence; the theory appeared obnoxious and meaningless not only in regard to the established institutions but also in regard to the problem of creating a new order.

These examples suffice to show how historical situations may work either for a theory of natural law or against it. The very notion of natural law—the meaning of the words "natural law"—is modified by historical and doctrinal contexts. Aristotle, the Stoics, Thomas Aquinas, Grotius, Tom Paine, and Adam Smith, for instance, had used and expounded the notion of natural law. But in their diverse systems of reference natural law has diverse, though not unrelated, meanings. When natural law is associated with individualistic attitudes and economic preoccupations, we can expect the words to mean something different from the "naturally just" (or adequate), τὸ δίκαιον, of Aristotle (*Ethics* 5.7.1134b18) or *jus naturale* of Aquinas. In an orderly preparation for the study of natural law, the most important step would be to list the main modifications undergone by the notion of natural law as a result of doctrinal and historical circumstances.

DIALECTIC AND HISTORY

We have been outlining a program of a dialectical and historical introduction to the study of natural law. In the introduction to a philosophic subject, dialectic and history should never be separated. A dialectic is a dialogue: it is the active statement of multiple views on a subject. So long as the dialogue continues, one does not know whether these views are thoroughly incompatible or can finally be reconciled and to what extent. We are best introduced to the analysis of a certain subject by considering the diverse views that can be held on it. But in order to have life, dialectic must be historical. One does not start by speculating that on such and such an issue four positions, say, A, B, C, and D are conceivable. Unless these positions are actually embodied in the history of ideas, one cannot know whether they are significant, whether they are the main relevant positions. Without history, A, B, C, and D may be no more than good-looking fabrications worked out by the desire to introduce in a question an appearance of order.

Writers of textbooks have a terrible habit of distributing possible answers under a number of types, each of which is designated by a name ending in "ism." Thus equipped with a list of words, some then do turn to history trying to find convincing illustrations of each type. But the type often vanishes in the search for a single significant expression of it in the actual history of thought, and much time has been wasted in ill-directed and misunderstood dialectical exercises. It should be done the other way around. The history of thought should be considered first, and the dialectical types should be disengaged from the experiments actually carried out by thinkers who have worked on the problem earnestly and perhaps with the inspiration of genius. The extraction of a dialectic from history, the working out of a dialectic substantiated by history, is a task incomparably more difficult than the construction of shadowy types which please the public by their artful way of observing the rules of symmetry in the performance of their roles. Unfortunately, dialectical constructions unsupported by history are found not only in textbooks but also in a few great books. Think, for instance, of the contrasted systems refuted by Bergson in *Time and Free Will* and in *Matter and Memory*. Who are those determinists, and who are those believers in free choice? Who are those subjectivists and idealists, those realists and materialists, those dogmatists, and those empiricists? [6]

Acquaintance with history never fails to improve the statement of philosophical questions. After all, the work of the great thinkers—as well as the spontaneous thinking of communities—is distinguished, with all its weaknesses and contradictions, by such genuineness and such profundity that better acquaintance with the history of their thoughts should forever remain the beginning of our dialectical approach. If we happen to discuss, for instance, the interpretation of freedom as indeterminacy, let us not be satisfied with names of systems. Let us quote Epicurus and Lucretius. Epicureanism was worked out not long after the death of Aristotle and it remained an influential and popular philosophy throughout the centuries. It is still very active in our time. But if the philosophy of Epicurus appeals so persistently to the human mind, it must be worth investigating. It certainly has a place in the dialogue of philosophers and it should be examined at its source.

It is hardly necessary to recall that the association of history and dialectic was initiated by Plato and by Aristotle. In order to follow the discussion of the causes in the first book of the *Metaphysics*, or to understand the first book of the treatise *On the Soul*, it is good to know both the Presocratics and Plato.[7] Whether the exposition of Aristotle is always historically correct is a problem. The historical expositions of Aristotle are the work of a dialectician, and the difficulties that they raise must be treated in relation to a dialectical purpose. It often happens that a thinker takes great trouble controlling, balancing, qualifying, and restricting a certain component of his thought. In spite of all precautions, the restricted component remains active and influential. Since the disciples have neither the skill nor the prudence of the great man, the restricted component of the teacher's thought sometimes quickly proceeds to the foreground of the dialectic scene, where it comes to bear the name of the man who was so eager to keep it balanced and qualified. In our time every new book on Rousseau evidences the concern to show that Rousseau has been misunderstood and did not actually uphold the theories famously connected with his name.[8] The truth probably is that these theories were held by Rousseau, but in the expressions of Rousseau himself they were balanced and qualified with the skill and, perhaps, the shrewdness of an artist of genius. As it enters history, the deep tendency of a certain thought is no longer protected by the skillful devices of its original interpreter, and it is in this unprotected condition that it plays its dialectical role. This holds for Rousseau; it may also hold, to some extent, for the Plato of Aristotle.

* * *

In the pages that follow we shall try to do at least two things: to see the difficulties where they are and to puncture a few myths. For, indeed, the history of ideas about natural law is crowded with myths. This accident is traceable principally to the fact that natural law, though a difficult philosophical problem, is also a subject of direct, intense, daily, and tragic interest to all sorts of people whose philosophic tools may well be primitive. One of the superiorities of the sciences over philosophy is that ordinary people are not supposed to have opinions on scientific matters. People generally do not argue about advanced mathematics, nuclear physics, or biochemistry. They may despise the men of science or reverence them, but they do not argue with them. Though it may not always be wholesome for scientists to talk exclusively among themselves, ordinary people simply have nothing to say on such subjects. But in philosophy, especially with regard to such problems as that of natural law, it is impossible—as well as undesirable—that argument be kept within the circle of professional philosophers. For one thing, philosophical questions, or many of them, concern all men. For another, there is in common intelligence a certain ability to approach and sometimes even to decide successfully some philosophical questions. In philosophy, the man of common intelligence is not expected to keep silent, he is not willing to, and sometimes at least he is plainly right. He is right because many issues of philosophic character concern him vitally. And if they concern him as a man of common intelligence, it should be possible to do something about them with the powers of common intelligence. How much is another question. The rate of failures will be high; especially, perhaps, when the non-philosopher is not just a man of common intelligence but also either a specialist or a man of action. This is inevitable because the ways of thought of such types are at variance with the philosophic disposition. A lawyer well-trained in legal matters, and in no other field, sometimes cannot avoid the philosophic problem of natural law. A revolutionary or a reformer or a politician who needs a theory to attack or criticize or defend the established order sometimes may be led into philosophizing about what is right and what is wrong by nature. In fact, much of the literature about natural law has been composed by legists and men dedicated to social and political action. But for a thorough analysis of natural law an elaborate technique and sharp philosophical instruments are needed; recall what was said about the problem of the unity of human nature and the antecedent problem of the universals. Now many men of great importance in the history of ideas about natural law had had only the most primitive, clumsy instruments for treating these problems. And no matter how intense their interest in the theory of natural law might have been, the use to which they put this theory was, more often than not, practical and historical. Under such circumstances, the proliferation of myths has been inevitable.

The History of Natural Law / 2

THE DISTINCTION between ideology and philosophy often proves a valuable instrument in the study of historical contexts in which certain general theoretical ideas have been discussed and worked out. Ideologies are by no means the only factors which significantly modify or even distort the actual elaboration of such subjects as that of natural law, but in many cases the relevant particularities of the historical treatment are best understood by being traced to the ideology of the time and the place. Now the theory of natural law may assume the character of philosophy or that of ideology, or it may combine philosophic and ideological features in various proportions; it is safe to say, however, that in most cases the powers of history have dragged it into the ideological condition, perhaps in spite of the philosophers' good will.

IDEOLOGY VERSUS PHILOSOPHY

According to the familiar use of the word, an ideology is a system of propositions which, though undistinguishable so far as expression goes from statements about facts and essen-

16

ces, actually refer not so much to any real state of affairs as to the *aspirations* of a *society* at a certain *time* in its evolution. These are the three components which, taken together, distinguish ideology from philosophy. The notion of truth which an ideology embodies is utilitarian, sociological, and evolutionistic. When what is actually an expression of aspirations assumes the form of statements about things, when these aspirations are those of a definite group, and when that group expresses its timely aspirations in the language of everlasting truth—then, without a doubt, it is an ideology that we are dealing with.

Let us consider a great example in American history. At the time of the Revolution it was commonly held that slavery was just a sorry remnant of the past and that it would silently disappear within a comparatively short period. The Constitution acknowledged slavery, but the Declaration of Independence had proclaimed the equality of all men and its universalistic principles inferred the emancipation of the slaves. Then, early in the nineteenth century, a celebrated machine, the mule-jenny, caused a sudden expansion of the cotton market and cotton production and made the institution of slavery appear more necessary than ever to a considerable part of the American society. In sharp contrast to the disposition which prevailed at the time of the Revolution, a slavery ideology was elaborated in the South. Among its proponents was John C. Calhoun, Vice-President of the United States from 1824 to 1832. In his pronouncements we find an exceptionally clear embodiment of the three features which distinguish ideology from philosophy. He expressed eloquently the aspirations of a certain society—viz., that part of the American people whose welfare depended on an abundant and cheap production of cotton. His eloquence was timely—the "peculiar institution" had come under severe attack. But Calhoun rested the ultimate justification of slavery on the premise asserting that since one portion of the community depended upon the labor of another portion, the former must unavoidably exercise control over the latter; this, he held, was a universal law of society.[1] Indeed, in order to fulfill its utilitarian, social, and historical function, an ideology must have the appearance of a philosophy and express itself in terms of universal truth. Sincerity is a thing which admits of many degrees, and if the adherents to an ideology did not believe with some sort of sincerity that they were adhering to incontrovertible facts and essential necessities, the ideology simply would not work.[2]

Not all ideologies are so easily identified or suffer the quick historical fate of the slavery ideology in the South of the United States. There are ideologies which express the aspirations of entire nations, or several nations, over long periods and under relatively stable historical circumstances. One could even say that there are ideologies expressive of ages or what are today called civilizations or cultures. To disengage the ideological features in these more complex cases, what is required is a sharper theoretical instrument than the more or less obvious material interest of a group at a given time in its history.

Scientifically, as well as logically, the weight of a proposition is an objective property, sometimes very easy and sometimes very hard to define and express. Suppose that in a long succession of trials a certain proposition p has been verified, with perfect regularity, ninety-eight times out of every hundred. The case is wonderfully simple, and all agree that the weight of p is defined and expressed by the ratio 98:100. But there can be a discrepancy between the scientific and logical weight of a proposition, on the one hand, and its psychological weight, on the other hand. Before p has been tested, or for the person unaware of the statistical data, the weight of p may either be totally indeterminate—this is the scientific attitude which treats the unknown as unknown—or it may be light, or heavy, or equal to one. If it is determinate, its determination proceeds from psychological or sociological factors, or from both. A person addicted to irrational fears, for instance, would attribute to the harmful occurrences an overwhelming probability, although he does not know what statistics say about the frequency of accidents. (He may even know that the ratio of accidents is extremely low, say, 1:10,000, and feel sure that his will be the wrong case; which, psychologically, is the same as to say that probability is one hundred percent and that the weight of p is absolute.) Examples of beliefs that are staunchly adhered to without objective evidence for the sole reason that they are held in common, taught by the community, and in a variety of ways guaranteed by it, are supplied in great abundance by folklore, superstition, and old wives' tales. In our time scientific enterprises depend so much upon teamwork conducted by society and certified by society, in a variety of ways and degrees of firmness, that the objective weight of proof and the sociological weight of common belief sometimes combine disquietingly. We sometimes wonder—this holds especially in medicine and psychology—whether the weight of unchallenged propositions is objective or, like that of old wives' tales, merely sociological.

The ambition of Auguste Comte was to achieve a strict coincidence of scientific objectivity and of sociological weight of all sorts of propositions and to pursue the "regeneration of human society" on the basis of unquestioned scientific dogmas. These were to be unquestioned not because the positive method delivers the mind's assent to the necessitating power of objectivity, but because the weight of the collective assent suppresses the freedom of movement on the part of the individual mind. When the development of research and theory made it clear to everyone that the weight of the "positive dogmas" was smaller than one, Comte was led to emphasize the importance of what we call the sociological weight, and his plans for a spiritual dictatorship became more definite.[3]

The campaigns of George Bernard Shaw against some dogmas of applied science express opposition to a sociological weight which is supposed to coincide with the weight of scientific objectivity but, in the author's mind, sometimes does not so coincide. Whatever the truth may be in the particular instances which aroused the fury of G. B. S., e.g., Jennerian vaccination, it was opportune to call attention to the danger of scientific superstition in an age in which science had become such a social affair.[4]

In dialectic as it is understood by Aristotle in the *Topics*, commonly accepted opinions play the part of axioms, but society, which thus supplies the first premises, acts as a witness and in this capacity connects the mind, no matter how imperfectly, with the universe of objectivity. The weight of a proposition asserted by all experts, or by most of them, or by the most highly reputed of them is only indirectly and imperfectly objective. Yet, inasmuch as the experts are reliable, the weight of dialectical premises is related to objectivity, as a result of which dialectic has the character of an introduction to science. The case of old wives' tales, whose weight is altogether sociological, is entirely different.

An ideology, precisely considered as such, is a system of propositions which carry a heavy sociological weight. Without an appearance of objectivity these propositions would have no weight at all; but their objective weight may be light or, in spite of appearances, nil, without their ideological function being impaired; *it may also be heavy*. Ideological propositions are not necessarily deceitful, although any truth entrusted to an ideology is exposed to all sorts of dangers. This circumstance entails significant consequences regarding the role of philosophers in society.

Between an ideology and a myth, in the sense of Sorel,[5] relations may be close. Yet the patterns imitated are different, and thereby ideology and myth are clearly distinct. Ideology imitates philosophy; it uses expressions principally relative to essential, intelligible, and everlasting necessities. A myth imitates the prediction of a fact, and by filling the minds and hearts of men with a certain anticipation it exerts an influence on the course of history, even though actual developments may be widely at variance with the fact anticipated.[6]

Finally, a utopia is characterized by a feature foreign both to the successful ideology and to the successful myth: as a construct worked out in the clarity of rational planning, it ignores contingency. Utopia does not spring from the actual trends of history and it cannot be realized without the destruction of a large amount of historical substance. This is why its realization demands the instruments of an irresistible power— e.g., that of an unchecked and totalitarian state.[7]

In contrast with ideology, the law of philosophy is altogether one of objectivity. The object of an aspiration is not a pure object; it is an object and it is something else, viz., an *end*, just as the object of transitive action is an *effect*. The object of cognition alone is a *pure object*: this is one of the best approaches to a definition of cognition.[8] It is by being an end (or a way to an end) that the thing desirable takes on the capacity of object in regard to desire, and it is by being an effect that the thing effected (or to be effected) takes on the capacity of object in regard to transitive action. The object of an ideology is, in spite of appearances without which the ideology would not work, an object of desire. The object of philosophy is a pure object.

Concerning relation to time, let it be said that philosophic disciplines, like all sciences properly so called, are concerned with intelligible relations and eternal laws of possibility. Any demonstration, insofar as it is faithful to its very exacting pattern, deals with eternal truth. The ratio of genuinely demonstrative reasonings that the human mind actually accomplishes in its endeavor to bring about science is a totally different issue. It is reasonable to hold that completely demonstrative inferences are few, both in philosophic and other sciences. These few are treasured, for they make up the soul of all that the human mind actually creates as it struggles toward the understanding of things.

In a consistent pragmatic philosophy, if such a thing were possible, the distinction between philosophy, which is characterized by objectivity and timelessness, and ideology, which is utilitarian and timely, would vanish. Philosophy would disappear into ideology. There would be no more philosophy, but few would be happy; and since pragmatism professes to uphold theories that "work," the pragmatists would not want to bring about a state of affairs which would make unhappy all philosophically-minded persons. In fact, some of the pragmatists (Peirce, James, Dewey . . .) are men of authentic philosophic genius. We can, therefore, expect the pragmatists to ensure that pragmatism remains inconsistent and that the philosophic intelligence is never denied a chance.[9]

It is now clear that keeping philosophy—a pursuit in which not philosophers alone are interested—free from the features proper to ideology is always, at best, a difficult and precarious achievement. A philosophy unaffected by any ideological feature would involve a degree of perfection that human affairs do not admit of. All that can be said is that some philosophies succeed better than others in preserving their law of objectivity against the ideological influences of the societies where they are conceived. One of the main reasons why the Greek philosophers of the great period remain our best teachers of philosophic fundamentals is that they have achieved distinguished success in the difficult task of transcending, for the sake of objectivity, the aspirations of their world.

Even if the sociological weight described in the foregoing happened to coincide with a heavy objective weight, ideological associations would make philosophic propositions undependable. Keeping philosophy "pure" is especially difficult in moral matters, and more particularly in subjects that concern directly and vitally the whole life of societies. Natural law is one of these subjects. A treatise on natural law which would be purely philosophic and in no way influenced by the ideological needs of the time is, in fact, almost impossible. Ideological currents will at least influence the choice of the questions treated; we shall be fortunate if they do not exert any perverse influence on the actual treatment of these questions.

Our time has witnessed a new birth of belief in natural law concomitantly with the success of existentialism, which represents the most thorough criticism of natural law ever voiced by philosophers. Against such powers of destruction we feel the need for an ideology of natural law. The current interest in this subject certainly expresses an aspiration of our society at a time when the foundations of common life and of just relations are subjected to radical threats. No matter how sound these aspirations may be, they are quite likely to distort philosophic treatments. For a number of years we have been witnessing a tendency, in teachers and preachers, to assume that natural law decides, with the universality proper to the necessity of essences, incomparably more issues than it is actually able to decide. There is a tendency to treat in terms of natural law questions which call for treatment in terms of prudence. It should be clear that any concession to this tendency is bound promptly to cause disappointment and skepticism. People are quick to realize what is weak, or dishonest, in pretending to decide by the axioms of natural law, or by airtight deduction from these axioms, questions that really cannot be solved except by the obscure methods of prudence,

and they gladly extend to all theory of natural law the contempt that they rightly feel toward such sophistry. Thus,
whereas an ideological current marked by relativistic and evolutionistic beliefs may cause a situation strongly unfavorable
to the theory of natural law, ideological currents expressive
of an eagerness to believe that some things are right and some
things wrong by nature may cause another kind of difficulty
and call for a supplement of wisdom on our part.

In spite of all the dangers of error to which every ideological
belief is exposed, let it be repeated that the content of an
ideology is not necessarily at variance with the truth of philosophy. The sociological weight which causes assent to ideological propositions may coincide with an objective weight pertaining to these propositions. What expresses the aspirations
of a society may also express a real state of affairs. That society
is blessed whose aspirations coincide with truth. No doubt
something can be done to promote such happy coincidence.
Something can be done to let the light of philosophical truth
into the visions that haunt the mind of societies and play a
role in the shaping of their destinies. Here we come to the
problem of the function of philosophers in society. Are there
circumstances in which philosophers are called to utter judgments about present events and trends and by public statements try to influence history?

It is important to realize at the outset that it is an illusion
to think that the concrete problems of action can be treated
by philosophic means. Even moral philosophy, practical philosophy, proceeds according to theoretical ways. When the
term of the comparison is unqualifiedly practical wisdom, the
wisdom of the man of action—in a word, prudence— the whole
of philosophic thought should be described as theoretical.[10]
To be sure, there is no essential reason why a theoretical
thinker should not be a statesman, but there are many accidental reasons why the association of such widely different

qualities will be exceptional. Just think of the human experience that the wisdom of the statesman indispensably requires; this experience is not acquired by spending the best of one's youth in public libraries. But is it possible to become proficient in philosophy without dedicating much of one's youth to the study of philosophic texts? The following question would be a fruitful approach to the heart of Platonism: precisely what principles and postulations are needed to bear out the proposition that the philosopher's training is the best possible preparation for the ruling of a state? The philosopher-king is plausible and necessary in the system of Plato, but a philosopher possessing the kind of experience and wisdom required for the government of a state is highly improbable in the real world.

And yet, under certain circumstances the direct cooperation of persons trained in philosophy may be desirable in the shaping of social or political events. Even if it be granted that a philosopher is restricted to abstractions and has no sense for political contingencies, he may sometimes contribute to the defense of public conscience against corruption by politicians and by intellectuals of a certain sophisticated sort. In the performance of such a task, which calls for the proper treatment of a few so-called "abstract ideas," e.g., those of right, law, community, authority, violence, legal coercion, autonomy, freedom, philosophic training is necessary or at least very helpful. The ideas about right, law, community, authority, etc., in any political situation are bound to be enmeshed in contingency and weighed down by ideology. A philosopher is not equipped to handle contingent matters and he probably can never fully escape the ideological influence of the society in which he lives. But a philosopher knows what prudence is; he knows what conditions must be satisfied for the handling of contingent matters to be prudential. And, even if he shares the aspirations of his society, a philosopher also realizes the importance of the stake that his society has in knowing the truth. Now, by providing standards by which it may be possible to distinguish between prudential action and sheer expediency, or between a good law and a bad one, a philosopher makes not an insignificant contribution. In order that the duties of prudence be fulfilled, more than a common sense ability to handle "abstract ideas" is sometimes required of the prudent, the statesman. The need for such ability is obvious when there is a question of contributing as much truth as possible to the visions which animate a community, to its role in mankind and history—to its *ideology*, if this word could be freed from all bad connotations.[11]

Communities, peoples, nations have a variety of vocations to fulfill, and it is normal and altogether desirable that each one be especially dedicated to certain aspects of the good that human communities ought to serve. There is much to be said for and against the factual accomplishments of the Spanish-speaking peoples, and there is much to be said for and against the accomplishments of the Anglo-Saxon peoples. But who would say that the historical calling of the Spaniards, *Hispanidad*, is the same as that of the Anglo-Saxons? A particular historical calling does not involve the lawless manipulation of essential truth as if, for instance, the calling of one people were to assert equal justice for all, and that of another people to insure the predominance of the tall, blond, dolichocephalic, nordic strain of men. But a special dedication to definite aspects of universal truth and justice, in harmony with the most precious contingencies of history, does constitute the vocation of a particular people. No doubt, a great deal of ability to handle "abstract ideas" is needed to formulate with appropriate emphasis, and with all the precautions against destructive exclusions, the aspect of the human good that a people is called to serve with unique dedication. It is too bad that philosophers should generally be so ill-prepared to understand the contingencies of political history, for their help is certainly needed to formulate, in a spirit of uncompromising objectivity, the visions which express and inspire the vocation of a people. In their more abstract aspects these visions can be termed ideologies. When emphasis is laid on historical actuality and anticipation, a good expression is that coined by Jacques Maritain: "concrete historical ideal." [12]

The revival of interest in natural law in our own time is certainly related to the devastations wrought by positivism and existentialism in the intellectual and political life of a considerable part of Western society, which—it is generally agreed —is undergoing rapid and radical transformations. By our own example, then, we realize how the theory of natural law may be influenced by the aspirations of a society at a certain moment of its evolution, and how great is the danger for that theory of becoming nothing more than an expression of these aspirations. As we go over the history of ideas on natural law, it is always relevant to ask whether or how far they are genuinely philosophical, or whether and how far they are merely ideological. With the understanding that a more thorough exposition remains desirable, it is legitimate to proceed by a succession of briefly treated historical examples. Clearly, nothing in the way of an historical survey is attempted here.

SOME EXAMPLES OF HISTORICAL ADVENTURES OF NATURAL LAW

Aristotle

Aristotle is one of the founders of the theory of natural law, although he did not carry its explicit development very far. There are some gaps in his metaphysics which make it difficult for him to elaborate on the foundations of finality and of law, either in physical nature or in mankind. This applies mostly to his uncertainties concerning the relation of this world to God. The God of Aristotle, first mover of the visible universe, is final cause of all that happens, moving all things in the capacity of an object of love. That much is certain. As to the question of whether God is also the efficient cause of becoming, and as to the question of whether he knows the world, the most that can be said is that the undeveloped and obscure expressions of Aristotle evidence a feeling of unsolved difficulty. Many historians of ideas will say, purely and simply, that Aristotle's God is not an efficient cause and that he does not know the world.[13] Such blunt negations are not borne out by unmistakable texts. It is more exact to say that Aristotle never worked out the metaphysical instruments necessary to understand God as efficient cause without having him bear the counter-impact of his own causation. Aristotle was unable to explain how God's cognition of the world involves no influence of things upon him, no passivity on the part of his intellect. When we consider the relation between natural law and intelligence, we realize that a metaphysician who lacks the instruments needed for treating the relation between natural law as a rule of behavior immanent in things and natural law as the judgment of an ultimate governing intelligence—we realize that such a metaphysician is reasonably inclined to economy of words on the subject.[14]

The greatest period of Greek philosophy, which ends with the death of Aristotle (322 B.C.), is distinguished by exceptional freedom from ideological influences and, more generally, from practical bias. When, in later periods, philosophy will again perform feats of theoretical disinterestedness, it will always be under the influence of the greatest thinkers of Greece, especially Plato and Aristotle. The philosophies of the East have never attained such a state of theoretical purity.

After the death of Aristotle, the Greeks themselves yield to the primacy of practical concern, and whereas Democritus is a straightforward philosopher of nature who proposes an explanation of natural events, Epicurus and his disciples are moralists who are determined to pattern the explanation of the physical world according to the requirements of their moral purposes. They generally follow the early Atomists in philosophy of nature, but when a physical view of Democritus does not suit their ideas on human happiness, Epicureans correct Democritus without any pang of conscience.* The primacy of the practical concern holds also for the greatest philosophy of the post-Aristotelian period—Stoicism.

To go back to Aristotle, let us remark that unqualified philosophic purity seems never to have been attained by any philosopher. With regard to such questions as slavery and manual labor, Aristotle is not as independent a thinker as he remains in so many other fields of inquiry. Thus, while his explanation of technique as intellectual habitus (*Ethics* 6.4.1140a) is a lasting contribution, on the subject of manual labor his mind seems to be overwhelmed with unreal pictures of separation between the skill of the hand and the technical judgment. And so it happens that Aristotle sometimes implies that he who uses his hands to shape physical nature according to human desires works out of routine and without rationality (*Metaphysics* 1.1.981a24). One is left to wonder whether the Greeks would have built the Parthenon and their other monuments if their architects had had no other manual help than that of brutes merely able to follow a tradition and to obey the impulses of routine. To account for the weaknesses of Aristotle in his discussion of labor and slavery, it is useful to observe the history of ideas about manual labor in the Greek world. The undervaluation of manual labor, which is conspicuous in Aristotle, seems to be a late development. One does not find it in Homeric society. The kings of Homer are farm-

---

* This applies principally to the swerve of the atom, *clinamen*, by which Epicurus gets rid of the "necessity of the natural philosophers," a thing he found still more uncongenial than the whims of gods and goddesses. See below, pp. 58-59.

ers who work with their laborers. Nausicaa, the daughter of a king, goes to the creek to wash the laundry with her maids. It is relatively late that manual labor comes to be held in such contempt. This depreciation of labor seems to be connected with the expansion of slavery. One might be tempted to believe that laborers were slaves because labor was despised and considered unworthy of a free man. But it seems that to some extent it may have happened the other way around, and that labor came to be despised after it had been associated with the condition of slavery.[15] And thus we have to confess that an ideological element is found in Aristotle himself. Even his philosophy—in part—is influenced and stained by an ideology which expressed the aspirations of a particular society at a particular time in its evolution. He endowed the free man with all the ambitions which in other societies distinguish the intellectual.

The Stoics

The contribution of the Stoics to the theory of natural law is of great significance, and in their case the historical context is extremely important. One of the most striking features of the Stoics' teaching in ethics is their universalism, their sense of human unity, their belief that human affairs are governed by rules that hold universally. The Stoics are citizens of the world, citizens of the human republic, and they are strongly inclined to believe in propositions that are equally true and good in all parts of the world. After Plato and Aristotle, they are the main founders of moral universalism.

The question of whether the universalism of the Stoics is connected with actual situations in political and social affairs certainly must be answered in the affirmative. The societies in which the Stoics of the three periods (Early, Middle, Late) live and teach are open and fluid. Stoicism takes shape a short time after the death of Aristotle. (Zeno was born in 322 B.C., the year of Aristotle's death.) Now, Aristotle had a famous pupil whose conquests brought a certain unity to territories extending from Macedonia to India. In Afghanistan, the cultural effects of the Alexandrian conquests are evidenced by an artistic marvel in the combination of Buddhist and Greek influences resulting in things of beauty which bear a bewildering likeness to Gothic forms. This culture supplies convincing evidence of an extraordinary broadening of social realities. Referring to the celebrated pages of Bergson on the closed and the open society, one may say that the society in which early Stoicism develops assumes, rather suddenly and on an exceptional scale, the characteristics of the open society.[16] The change brought about by the Macedonian conquest contrasts sharply with the preceding order of the city-states. It is reasonable to hold that Stoic universalism—so important in the evolution of ideas about natural law—is determined to a large extent by needs resulting from an unprecedented amount of communication among most diverse cultures. Between the foundation of the Stoic school by Zeno and the death of Marcus Aurelius (180 A.D.), there is a span of nearly five centuries. The society in which Stoicism is influential remains fluid, of huge dimensions, and extremely liberal as far as what we would call today national and racial particularities are concerned. These later phases of antiquity are marked by the extraordinary power of assimilation which characterizes Greek and Latin culture and Roman administration.

Roman Law

The development and organization of Roman law, throughout the history of the Roman Empire, constitute subjects of obvious relevance for the interpretation of ideas on natural law. We want merely to recall here that the law of the Romans, unlike the common law of the Anglo-Saxons, is a written law. This contrast will raise interesting problems. In the Anglo-

Saxon countries natural law will be thought of in relation to an unwritten positive law made of precedents and of traditions, rather than in relation to principles elaborated by theoretically-inclined thinkers. A theory of natural law growing in a context of unwritten common law and a theory of natural law growing in a context of written Roman law are likely to be quite different, if not in their essence, at least in their expression. To locate the development of Roman law in history, let us recall the name of Gaius (whose main works were composed between 130 and 180 A.D.), that of Ulpian (main works, 211-222), and that of Justinian (publication of the *Digest*, 533).

Scholasticism

Another historical context of great importance for the theory of natural law is the codification of canon law effected about 1140 A.D. by Gratian in a work known as *Concordia discordantium canonum* or *Decretum Gratiani*. We are now in the so-called scholastic period. If we are also on our way to puncture a few myths, the time has come to deal with a big one: the myth of "scholastic doctrine," one of the most obnoxious that has ever plagued the history of thought. Strikingly, it is only in the last twenty years or so that the best informed people have come to know this myth for what it is. The truth of the matter is that in the so-called scholastic period one or two dozen doctrines clash violently with each other. Scholastic philosophy is a myth, as ill-grounded and mischievous as the myth of "contemporary philosophy."

One often hears beginners (and sometimes older people who have retained the psychology of beginners) declare: "Contemporary philosophy holds. . . ." The philosophy of our time is thus credited with some degree of doctrinal unity. But as soon as we look for an unquestionable representative of a unified body of doctrine which could be called contemporary philosophy, we are confronted by a multiplicity of conflicting philosophies all of whom have an equal right to be considered contemporary. Who is more of a contemporary philosopher, Henri Bergson or Bertrand Russell? Bergson was born in 1859 and Russell in 1872. Bergson died in 1941 and Russell is still doing well in 1965. Russell thoroughly despises the work of Bergson, but Bergson, who was an exquisitely courteous man, never let it be known what he thought of Russell. It would be completely arbitrary to say that one is more than the other a philosopher of our time. Or consider such thinkers as Carnap and Heidegger: have they not an equal right to be included among the philosophers of the twentieth century in spite of their divergencies?

Scholasticism lacks doctrinal unity as certainly as contemporary philosophy does. The adjective "scholastic" can be relevantly predicated of a few things, but not of a doctrine. It can be relevantly predicated of a language: scholastic Latin is very different from classical Latin and from the cultured Latin that the Humanists of the Renaissance would write. It can be predicated of a set of problems: in German, *eine Problematik*. Certain questions belong, and other questions definitely do not belong, to the scholastic *Problematik*. "Scholastic" can also be predicated of a method of research and exposition. Finally, it can be predicated of certain frames of mind, of some mental habits. When a thinker who uses scholastic Latin, studies scholastic problems, and follows the scholastic method confesses that a certain situation can be affected by accident, do not expect him to appreciate the frequency or the volume of the accident. His tendency, whether expressed or not, is to assume that accidents are few. This is not a doctrinal issue; it is an issue pertaining entirely to the psychology of knowledge and the psychology of teaching. In this capacity, however, it assumes great importance in the understanding of the existential man. When we set in contrast the Scholastics and the Humanists of the Renaissance, we do not mean only that the latter write better Latin than the former; we also imply that the Humanists show a readiness to acknowledge the huge dimensions of accidental occurrence and consequently have an ability to achieve a concrete and historical understanding of man. Such readiness and ability are generally absent from whatever is called scholasticism.

With regard to natural law, to speak of "the scholastic doctrine" is nonsensical and misleading. Thomas Aquinas (1225-1274) is as much of a Scholastic as anyone can be, and he has a doctrine of natural law. But what about William Occam (1300-1349)? He also is a Scholastic, but he holds that the quality of our actions is entirely determined by arbitrary decrees of the divine will, nothing being right or wrong by nature. According to Gallus M. Manser, for Occam "all depends on the divine will as ultimate cause—the essences of things, the possible and the impossible." There are no unchangeable laws, nothing right or wrong in itself: ". . . theft, adultery, and even hating God are not wrong in themselves, for God can command them, and then they become meritorious." [17] For Thomas Aquinas such words are sheer blasphemy. (*De Veritate*, XXXIII, 6.)

Renaissance and After

When we come to the Renaissance, the historical context of the greatest significance is the emergence of the secular society. According to popular belief, medieval theories of the state are theocratic, representing the civil society as contained in the spiritual society and devoid of autonomy. In fact, open professions of theocracy seem to constitute extreme and infrequent cases in the Middle Ages. Nevertheless, it is probably safe to say that the vision of a fully unified society—one in which the duality of the spiritual and the temporal would be reduced to a minimum—is haunting the medieval mind.

(Vague expressions are here being used in order to make allowance for the extreme variety of circumstances which are covered when we dare speak of such an ill-defined thing as the Middle Ages.) What is certain is that in the sixteenth century secular societies assert their autonomy with more firmness and, on the whole, with more success than before. And as it often happens that opposite trends gain power simultaneously, the tendency toward various sorts of theocratic states may have been stronger in the age of the Renaissance than in the Middle Ages.

Among the jurists, the name most commonly associated with the movement toward a more independent temporal society is that of Hugo Grotius (1583-1645), a theorist of natural law and of international law. Natural law and international law are often associated for obvious reasons. As long as there is no organized international community, there is no written law and little customary law in international affairs. Therefore, in this domain we depend much more than elsewhere on agreement about what is just by nature. Grotius was not an atheist (he was a believing Protestant), but he did not miss a chance to emphasize the autonomy of nature: "Even if, contrary to all my belief, there were no God, there would still be natural laws of the right and the wrong." [18]

Notice that there is nothing particularly democratic about this emergence of secular societies; it is concomitant to or quickly followed by the trend toward absolute monarchy, a trend which was successfully held in check in England but not so successfully elsewhere. And with the period of absolute monarchies, the theory of natural law enters into a new context. In order to bear out the monarchs' claim to absolutism, the supporters of absolute monarchy speak of the divine right of kings. The expression "divine right" is exceedingly ambiguous, and its ambiguity has caused and is causing much confusion and error in political theory.[19] It may mean anything, from the common view that the claim of a man to the obedience of another man is null and void unless it is ultimately grounded in God, to the extreme position of Filmer (*Patriarcha*, 1680), holding that kings are historical successors to the Patriarchs, who are successors to the sons of Noah, who are successors to their father, himself the historical successor of Adam who was designated by God to rule the human race. Despite such confusion, one thing remains certain: at the time of the absolute monarchies the theories of divine right mean that the king is in no way accountable to the people. Accordingly, the theory of natural law becomes a vindication of the natural right of the people against the alleged divine right of the king. And the notion of natural law is frequently associated with two particular concepts designed to hold in check the absolutistic tendencies of the monarchies, viz., the concept of a state of nature antecedent to the state of society and that of a contract between the people and the governing personnel. These concepts are not new, but it is easy to see how they can be deeply modified by the very fact that they play an active part in the ideology of a society struggling against absolutism. Words carry great power and the word "natural" becomes a new historical force when "natural right" and "natural law" are engaged in a belligerent opposition to "divine right."

The Classical Economists

Observing the prevailing practices, the founders of the "orthodox" science of economics were overwhelmed by the conviction that progress in production and distribution was crippled by feudal rights, customs, and barriers, guild constitutions, company charters, and obsolete regulations of every description. Now all these restraining factors are man-made, and against man-made dispositions which prove harmful minds tend to appeal to nature. The man-made and the natural are thus set in opposition, with an inescapable implication that the man-made is unnatural. Even society, after all, is the result of human dispositions; only the individual, with his desires and his practices fair or foul, is the true expression of nature. The natural order is characterized by individualism; so let people deal in the market place, sell if they find buyers, and purchase if they can afford the prices. Let the state keep its hands off. Abolish anything which restricts the operation of economic particles; they are guided by "an invisible hand." Here an essentially corpuscular theory of economic life becomes identified with the "scientific" determination of natural law and natural order. And there still are people who consider it altogether unnatural that prices or wages should be influenced by governmental regulation or by the concerted action of unions and consumer associations. In order to understand the historical power of the atomistic interpretation of the natural order by the founders of the classical school of economics, we must realize that the release of individual energies was their most effective way of getting rid of obsolete institutions.

Socialism and Historical Right

The association of the "natural order" with the most thorough individualism is an accident of the very first magnitude in the evolution of ideas about nature and society. In this vision of the natural order, kept alive by generations of economists, "natural" is understood in opposition both to "rational," "planned out," and to "historical." The calling of socialism, ever since the beginning of the nineteenth century, has been to discover rational institutional forms flexible enough to accommodate the swiftly changing circumstances of production and distribution in the industrial society. In spite of its connections with romanticism, socialism often embodies an opposition to "nature." To understand the meaning of this opposition we must consider that socialism has been and, to a large extent, remains a reaction against the individualistic naturalism of classical economists. In socialism the search for wise, rational, scientific ways of social reorganization is historically connected with opposition to the concept of an atomistic society in which the natural order is expected to emerge without the cooperation of wisdom.

The individualistic notion of the natural order is also opposed by diverse schools of thought dedicated to the meaning and worth of history's creations. Any individualistic exaltation of the natural order sets nature in opposition to history and places the creations of history under constant threat of destruction, whether violent or gradual. The notion of historical right, as opposed to natural right, was made famous by the German jurist Friedrich Carl von Savigny (1779-1861).

The tendency to oppose a philosophy of historical right to a philosophy of natural right is active mostly in conservative movements throughout the nineteenth century. But when the criticism of natural law combines a keen sense and a high valuation of history with socialistic thought and action, the result is George Sorel and a few other eccentrics. It is reliably said that these eccentrics had something to do with the training of Mussolini.

Racism

The last historical context to be mentioned here is constituted by contemporary racism. Notice that ever since the Renaissance and the conquest of the world by the white man racism has been popular, for obvious reasons. Old wives' tales about the inequality of races, which occasionally assumed a theological appearance in the sixteenth century, became "really scientific" in the nineteenth and twentieth centuries. The explosion of racist feeling in the 1930s and 1940s need not be specially recalled. Today racism is very active in several parts of the world but its positions, although still very strong, are mostly defensive. It no longer enjoys the unique power which pertains to visions that claim to lead precisely where history goes. Revived interest in the universalism of natural law is partly due to a reaction against the evil perpetrated during the period of racist predominance.[20]

* * *

Let it be said once more that the eagerness to believe in natural law which is evident in a part of our society may occasion oversimplifications, unwarranted generalizations, and all sorts of illusions quickly conducive to skepticism. For the theorist of natural law, this favorable disposition makes it even more necessary to seek the highest degree of theoretical purity. A theorist is always in danger when he feels that there is in his public a "will to believe" which, if needed, is ready to supplement the insufficient clarity of his analysis and overlook for a while possible gaps in his demonstrations. Considering again the role of philosophers in society, it must be granted that the circumstances which render a certain doctrine particularly timely may be such as to admit of no delays. When souls devastated by skepticism, desperation, and meaninglessness express their willingness to believe that the universe of morality is not merely a tale told by an idiot, philosophers would fail in their function if they requested these eager souls to wait until definitions are perfect, deductions strict, and axioms expressed in uncontrovertible formulas. The appropriate behavior may be described as a movement back and forth between the kind of thought and expression that the state of society and souls urgently requires and the condition of theoretical purity and intelligible lucidity, which can be approached only very slowly and only through many trials and errors. Unless the movement toward historic timeliness (what French intellectuals today call *la pensée engagée*), is quickly followed by a return to the sources of disengaged, independent thought, the most fruitful philosophical propositions soon take on the deadly condition of clichés. A striking example is supplied by the adventures of "personalism" in the last generation. If several schools of personalistic philosophy attracted so much attention after the end of the first World War, it was not without very good historical reasons. At a time when the everlasting tendency of human societies to achieve order by the predominance of functions over such subjects as the small community, the family, and ultimately the person; at a time when the individualism of the preceding ages had proved definitively inadequate and powerless—at such a time the circumstances of history clearly called for new developments in the philosophical understanding of the person.[21] But personalistic clichés have confused many things. Any proposition causes confusion and error as soon as it becomes a cliché. Clichés are obnoxious for a number of reasons but principally because they make things look clear and easy, because they render people unable to perceive the depth of difficulties. In brief, they kill the sense for mystery. Similarly, propaganda at the service of natural law is apt to make people believe that the things right or wrong by nature are easily determined and explained. One of the social functions of philosophers, when they speak of natural law, is to remind men that their own nature, the moral nature, the universe of morality, is no less mysterious than this physical universe.

Some Theoretical Questions /3

INDEFINITELY many theoretical issues would valuably contribute, if clarified, to the understanding of natural law. In this doctrinal matter, as well as in the historical matter of the preceding chapter, the best we can hope for is to exercise some skill in the selection and description of a few examples.

THE CONCEPT OF NATURE

We have already remarked that the understanding of natural law may be thoroughly impaired by failure to treat the logical and critical question of the universal. Here let us consider first a related subject, viz., the concept of nature. When Aristotle speaks of the "natural just," τὸ δίκαιον φυσικόν, and sets it in opposition to the "legal just," τὸ δίκαιον νομικόν, (*Ethics* 5.7.1134b18) let us be aware that the notion of the just, such as Aristotle conceives it, is not exclusively ethical, is not confined to the order of morality. The "just" (and not only in Greek) is the adjusted, the adequate, that which fits exactly in a relation to something else. When Aristotle speaks of that which is just by nature, he refers to a concept of nature which transcends the order of voluntary action. In other words, the "natural just" of Aristotle—and the same remark holds, by all means, for the natural right and the natural law of Thomas Aquinas—ignores the particular meaning that we often attribute to the contrast between the physical and the moral worlds. Between the two communication is insured not only by the notion of nature but also by that of justice, which fundamentally signifies adjustment.* These relations have been obscured and made almost inconceivable by the modern development of mechanism and idealism. Recalling what was said in the first chapter about the skill of great thinkers in balancing and keeping under control the paradoxical components of their systems, it should be said that the commentators on Kant are doing their job when they insist that notions relative to nature and to what is good for nature are not absent from the work of Kant. But when that necessary job is completed, the fact remains that Kant (1724-1804) is the philosopher who expressed, with more sharpness and consistency than any of his predecessors, the contrast between nature and morality. The meaning of this contrast, its extent, and its rank in ethical and legal philosophy, are things which cannot be taken for granted and whose examination is obviously of decisive relevance for the study of natural law.[1]

Nature, in the physics of Aristotle, signifies entity, essence, whatness, quiddity with a constitutional relation to action,

---

* Under the influence of biological patterns, our contemporaries have made the word adjustment one of their favorite expressions, and in contexts in which men of the Kantian era would have used, as a matter of course, moral and moralistic terms, many people speak today quite naturally of adjustment and adaptation. Does this mean that genuinely moral ideas are being displaced by ideas taken over, within a system of naturalistic postulates, from the natural sciences? This is, no doubt, one aspect of the case. But the same facts also reveal a movement away from the Kantian frame of mind, and this movement points to new possibilities for the understanding of communications and continuities between nature and morality.

operation, movement, growth, development. A nature is a way of being which does not possess its state of accomplishment instantly but is designed to reach it through a progression. (*Phys.* 2.1. 192b, *Met.* 5.4. 1014b.) There are broad domains of knowledge where the notion of nature with its distinctive dynamism plays no role, and these domains exercise an everlasting attraction on all parts of human science. It has always been difficult to define logic and to define mathematics; in our time achieving such definitions is commonly reputed impossible. Some consider this state of affairs agonizingly painful, others are resigned to it and think that they still can enjoy life and do good work in logic and in mathematics without being able to say what these are all about. One thing on which all would be agreed is that the treatment of mathematics has undergone deep changes, especially since the time when Kant felt entitled to write that geometry had remained such as it was shaped by Euclid, and the time when Legendre said that the *Elements* of Euclid were an airtight system in which it was impossible to find any flaw. Legendre died in 1833; then, Lobachevsky was forty years old. The development of non-Euclidean geometrics (Lobachevsky, 1793-1856, Bolyai, 1802-1860, and Riemann, 1826-1866), was only the first in a series of revolutionary events which have brought about a representation of mathematics widely at variance with that of Euclid and Archimedes and even with that of Descartes or Kant or Legendre. But despite all the bewildering transformations that we are alluding to, mathematics, which played the role of guiding star in the whole universe of science at the time of Plato and Aristotle, still plays this role today. Another remarkable fact is that, in the modern as well as in the ancient conception, a mathematical entity is not a nature. The formalist majority and the intuitionist minority in modern mathematics would agree that a mathematical object, whatever it may be, is not a nature in the sense defined above, and that, whereas we may call it, if we please, essence, whatness, quiddity, etc., we may not attribute to it a dynamism, a tendency to forge its way in a world of becoming. It does not grow; it is what it is by definition, by construction, instantly; it is possessed of its proper condition of accomplishment immediately and does not have to acquire it by growth. No wonder that the psychology of the botanist is widely different from that of a mathematician, for plants grow, and their full development never coincides with their initial condition. Here also there are entities, essences, whatnesses, quiddities, no matter how wretched our definitions and how deficient our information about the evolution of species. Plant a maple seed and if you claim that it grows into an oak tree no one in the world will believe it. And if a hundred witnesses swear to the truth of your case history the consensus will be that these are jokers without talent for good jokes, or that they are subject to pathological delusions. Again, we are not very good at defining living species and we know little about their evolution. Yet when we speak of maple trees and of oak trees, we are sure that we are speaking of whatnesses whose law of accomplishment is one of progression. Such whatnesses are natures in the sense of Aristotle.*

---

* It is not by chance that our exemplification of the concept of nature is taken from the world of living things: the properties of nature manifest themselves under conditions of distinguished clarity in the case of natures endowed with life. Such choice of examples should by no means convey the suggestion that the concept of nature holds only for the living and that, in order to apply it to inanimate things, these have to be fictitiously attributed some sort of life, as if any generalized interpretation in terms of nature had to be animistic (whether outspokenly or not). The physics of Aristotle has often been characterized as the work of a biologist who generalizes the patterns of explanation found successful in the treatment of the living. No doubt the fundamental patterns used by Aristotle in the explanation of nature are derived from the clearer case, which is that of living things. But Aristotle, at least in the period of his maturity, the period of the treatises which make up the *Corpus aristotelicum*, is entirely free from the tendency to attribute life

Among the implications of the concept of nature, we call attention to these three: plurality, teleology, and relation between beginning and end. The plurality of natures is one of the first questions treated by Aristotle in the *Physics*. Parmenides stands in the background; rightly or wrongly he was credited with a theory of absolute unity of the universe. According to the traditional interpretation, motion and plurality in the system of Parmenides are illusions; the world of reality is made of one single, large, definitely corporeal, motionless thing, without qualities, and without any other diversity than that resulting from the fact that its parts are external to each other. Any diversity in the world of Parmenides—as interpreted traditionally—is of quantitative character, and this picture of the world is the background of Aristotle's study of nature. But the Parmenidean world picture expresses the ideal, as well as the contradictions, of an everlasting mechanism.[2] For instance, Descartes also is a paradoxically thorough mechanist, at least as far as corporeal reality is concerned. He admits of only two substances, the thinking one and the extended one; in other words, consciousness and space. Should we say that in Descartes all natures are reduced to two? But consciousness, as understood by Descartes, can hardly be called a nature, and Cartesian space is not a nature in any conceivable sense: it is not a thing endowed with a constitutive identity by reason of which it would tend toward a state of accomplishment to be reached through a progression. The truth is that there are no natures in the universe of Descartes. Stability in natural processes, not being guaranteed by any nature, has to be guaranteed by an extrinsic power, and this

---

to all things. What Aristotle possibly failed to realize is that explanations in terms of nature, which work brilliantly in the clearer case of the living things, are of much more restricted power in the obscure domain of inanimate things and non-vital properties where it will be necessary to make a wide use of mechanistic abstractions, of constructs and beings of reason.

is how the theory of divine immutability comes to play an essential part in Cartesian physics: the laws of motion are such as we know them not by reason of any necessity immanent in things, but because God once decided that they would be such. Do not worry: God is not subject to whims, and He will not change his mind; the science of physics is possible.[3]

For Aristotle the plurality of physical natures is an obvious fact. Now when somebody denies an obvious fact or a self-evident principle he cannot be refuted by demonstration, for it is not possible to demonstrate the obvious. What is possible is to draw the consequences of his denial and to corner him either into confession of the obvious or into silence. Against Parmenides Aristotle draws the consequences of the monistic reduction:

> But if all things are one in the sense of having the same definition, like 'raiment' and 'dress,' then it turns out that they are maintaining the Heraclitean doctrine, for it will be the same thing 'to be good' and 'to be bad,' and 'to be good' and 'to be not good,' and so the same thing will be 'good' and 'not good,' and man and horse; in fact, their view will be, not that all things are one, but that they are nothing. . . . (*Physics* 1.2. 185b19, trans. R. P. Hardie and R. K. Gaye).

In the context of morality, to say that all things are one "in the sense of having the same definition" would entail that killing a horse and killing a man have about the same meaning. We have not demonstrated the fact that there exists a plurality of natures, but we have shown that denying such plurality entails unacceptable consequences. "Unacceptable," here, should not be understood practically or pragmatically or emotionally, but rationally. The thing rationally unacceptable helps to perceive an obviousness which happened not to be perceived directly.

* * *

Wherever there is nature there is direction toward a state of accomplishment, and in order to get rid of teleological considerations mechanism has first to replace nature by something else, e.g., extension. Who questions that an acorn and an oak tree are related as nature folded and nature unfolded, as nature in its initial condition and nature in its accomplished condition? In fact, we never speak of acorns and oak trees without postulating the teleological principle, and more precisely the physical form of this principle, i.e., the proposition that such things as acorns or infants are essentially related to a state of accomplishment to be achieved through progression. It would be exceedingly difficult to speak of acorns and oak trees, infants and adults without assuming that this proposition is obvious. But here we run into the kind of difficulty which always confronts us when we speak of obvious propositions. If a proposition is so clear, why does it not cause unanimous assent? How is it that almost every time a biologist speaks of teleology, he calls this notion all sorts of names: primitive, archaic, pre-scientific, foreign to science, anti-scientific? Then he would look at his watch and say, "Goodbye, I have to go to the dentist," which implies that teeth have a function to fulfill and that they can fulfill their function satisfactorily or not—and thus we are back to a firm belief in finality. When we are confronted by a denial that is as stubborn as it is paradoxical, a denial that is unflinchingly maintained although no one can live up to it either in action or in thought, it is always enlightening to inquire into its reasons. The reasons why teleological notions are held suspicious by the scientific mind are numerous. One of the most profound is already familiar to us: there are no natures and no final causes in mathematics. When we watch a geometrical figure or an equation develop its properties, we are aware that it is not in order to achieve a better state of affairs that this equation or this figure is effecting this development. Indeed, "effecting" is here purely metaphorical. The properties of a mathematical essence are not effected by this essence, they are identical with it and all the development takes place in our mind. Accordingly, whenever the interpretation of nature is mathematical, and insofar as it is mathematical, final causes are out of the picture. This is not an accident, and no misunderstanding is involved. The exclusion of final causes from every science where mathematical forms predominate follows upon the laws of mathematical abstraction and intelligibility.

It is easy to see what the consequences are for a problem like that of natural law. When the Cartesian universe displaces the universe of Aristotle, when a universe made of natures is displaced by a single huge thing, extension, whose parts and their arrangements and re-arrangements lend themselves beautifully to mathematical treatment, we have to deal with a world picture in which teleological considerations are as irrelevant as considerations of color and taste would be in geometry.[4] Of course, we are here supposing an ideal condition that mechanistic science has never actually attained. In the youthful ambition of Descartes this condition was to be realized quickly, and he meant what he said when he wrote the famous words, "I do not accept in my physics any principles that are not accepted in mathematics."[5] In its factual development, the modern science of nature—in all its parts but especially when it has to deal with living things—has continued to accept a few principles which have nothing to do with mathematics, principles connected with the notion of nature such as it was worked out by the Greeks and best expounded by Aristotle. With all our mechanistic good will, a chemical remains a thing ready to bring about definite effects under definite circumstances. Do you recognize a discreet expression of finality in this notion of readiness? This is how we keep arguing about teleology.

In Descartes, mechanism is accompanied by a spiritualistic

interpretation of all psychical processes in man. (In man alone, for animals are described as machines which react to stimulations but have no sensations and no feelings.) [6] There is no reason to cast doubt on the sincerity of Descartes' spiritualistic interpretation of human "thought"—a word which, in his system, covers all processes irreducible to arrangements of extension. But this daring spiritualist remains, as far as the physical universe is concerned, a uniquely thorough and uninhibited mechanist. He had the audacity of youth; he died relatively young and he lived (1596-1650) at the beginning of an era—in fact, our era. These beginners have optimistic views, great expectations, a certain naïveté, that those who come later hardly can afford. After Descartes one does not often find such a blunt, such a completely uninhibited expression of a mechanistic world picture. For Descartes, to say that the oak tree and the corn plant are natures different from each other is philosophically nonsensical. Such language is adequate in the art of farming and in the art of forestry but not in philosophy. An oak tree is an arrangement of extension, and a corn plant is another arrangement also of extension. And one-half of man—though not the better one—belongs to space just as certainly as a corn plant or an oak tree. It is not in any provisional way but in the most definitive sense that Descartes' philosophy of man is dualistic. Indeed, consciousness seems to move the portion of space that we call our body, and impressions made upon the body seem to determine other impressions in consciousness according to a law of one-to-one correspondence. But let us be honest and say that in Descartes those relations are unintelligible. [7] After Descartes, Spinoza (1632-1677) conceives one substance developing along two parallel lines, that of consciousness and that of extension, and the unity of the substance in which these lines originate supplies some sort of an explanation for the facts of one-to-one correspondence just alluded to. [8] In Leibnitz (1646-1716) the doctrine of pre-established harmony takes care of the questions raised and left unanswered by the dualism of Descartes. The world of consciousness and the world of extension are like two clocks; neither acts upon the other, but both were set by a wise horologer and when one strikes twelve so does the other.[9] Plainly, these are arbitrary hypotheses; yet they may be the best that philosophical genius can do after having split nature into consciousness and extension.

It goes without saying that there cannot be such a thing as natural law in a thoroughly mechanistic universe. When mechanism is associated with idealism, as it is in Descartes and in most modern philosophers—again, whether outspokenly or not—we have *values* instead of natural laws. Apparently, it is after having played a role of enormous importance in the work of the economists that the notion of value has reached the foreground, the most brightly lighted place in ethical philosophy. A realistic notion of value is not impossible; in a recent book Jacques Maritain did much to show what it would mean.[10] But in the actual history of modern and contemporary philosophy, values have generally been conceived as placed in things, imposed upon them, forced into them by the human mind. Assuming that we still retain a sense for the distinction between the right and the wrong, what else can we do if things have no nature and no finality of their own? The idealism of the value theory is generally subjectivistic; this is the case, especially, when the ethical theory of values is influenced by the speculations of the economists. In schools of economics it is commonly held that the value of a thing is determined not at all by its relation to good human life but entirely by the willingness of men to pay a certain price for the possession or use of that thing. From a certain standpoint it could be held very reasonably that food rich in carbohydrates and proteins is more valuable than, say, alcohol. Yet it seems to be a lasting convention among economists that the greater value simply coincides with the greater eagerness on the part of the consumer, so that if the majority is ready to sacrifice their biologically normal ration of carbo-hydrates and proteins in order to procure their full ration of vodka then all we can say is that vodka, in this particular district, has the greater value. Still, in order to understand the history of modern thought, and a few philosophic subjects, we must be aware that there is such a thing as a nonsubjectivistic idealism. Working out such an idealism was the task to which Kant dedicated his life, at least from the time he discovered the principles of criticism.[11] Subjectivistic interpretations of Kant are common—and plausible enough—but actually erro-neous. Kant was too much of a philosopher and too honest a man to produce just another system of subjectivistic ideal-ism; he dedicated the best of his efforts to reinterpreting the notion of scientific object. Whether he succeeded is another question. At any rate, when we hear today of moral values, esthetic values, social values, political values, spiritual values, etc., we should know where these come from. They come from the mind, they come from outside the things, they are not embodied in entities, in nature. Thus, "this has value" does not mean that by reason of what the thing is it is adjusted to something else, to some operation or to some relation: its value is something assigned to it by the mind while, in itself, it remains without value, without nature.

*　*　*

The opposition of beginning and end is relevant in all con-sideration of nature. This follows from the relation of essence to development when an essence is a nature. When we say of something that it is natural, when we speak of a natural con-dition, of the state of nature, etc., we may be referring to either part of an opposition or to both, and the meaning of our expressions has to be made unmistakable by the context.

We may be speaking of an incipient state of affairs where there is already a tendency toward a state of accomplishment; we may be speaking of the state of accomplishment itself; and we may be lumping together these two conditions. To explain, let us be permitted the use of an appalling hypothesis which, unfortunately, is not excluded from realization by any known necessity. Suppose that a hydrogen bomb, God forbid, should fall on a city, for instance, Chicago. Over and above the destruction wrought by the explosion and radiation, we must expect something unusual and unpleasant to happen. If only one million people are dead or helplessly wounded, some three million people would still be able to come and go, but they would quickly revert to a state of nature. For all practical purposes there would be no mayor, no police, no courts, no administration, and the plundering of wrecked houses would begin immediately. We would then realize for the first time what a blessing it is to live in a society which, despite setbacks of every description, operates with some sort of normality. In contrast to the state of society in which we are existing now, what we are imagining may be called a state of nature. By reason of the law of development embodied in every nature, "natural" can be predicated of either of these opposites: the initial, the incipient, the primitive, the native, the rudimentary, and the terminal, the final, the accomplished, the perfect. Which one is more natural for man: the nasty and brutish individualism which would follow the collapse of social structures or the relative social integration that we enjoy in a city where no more than about one person a day is shot down? It is instructive once in a while to stop and think of this amazing feat of civilization. Here are four million people from all parts of the world; they have excellent reasons to hate each other, and yet no more than about one a day is murdered. The state of civilization is much more in agreement with human nature than the circumstances which would prevail if the social structure suddenly broke down and plunderers and other criminals got loose or were checked only by casual defense. No doubt, a state of accomplishment is the most natural condition of a nature, for it is that toward which nature has been striving from the beginning and by reason of its identity with itself. Yet, in human affairs principally, the condition that nature is striving toward is not brought about by nature alone but requires such causes as understanding, crafts, arts, sciences, techniques, and above all, good will and wisdom.*

Should it be said that the use of "nature" and "natural" in these opposite senses is an intolerable case of ambiguity and that we should, by all means, have two words to express such distinct ideas? Other things being equal, what makes for distinct understanding is always preferable to what makes for confusion. But other things may not be equal: they are not when the distinct and even opposite meanings are related, and when perceiving their relation happens to be of great significance. All the dynamism of nature would be missed if our language did not remind us of the relation between the initial and the terminal, the rudimentary and the accomplished, the natural in the sense of that which is just given by nature antecedently to knowledge, craft, and wisdom, and the natural as that which implies the work of intelligence, experience, good will, wisdom, society. If we are going to use two words to convey these distinct and opposite but related meanings,

---

* Principally, and not exclusively, because in physical nature—as well as in human affairs—many realizations are either rare and precarious or unheard of except by the cooperation of human art. For example, chemistry is responsible for the constitution of innumerable compounds never produced, as far as we know, except under laboratory or industrial conditions, and there are many varieties of plants and animals not simply *found* in nature.

these words also should be related. There is an essay by de Bonald (1754-1840), a traditionalist and a critic of Rousseau, which is entitled "On the Native State and on the Natural State." [12] In some contexts at least, "native" and "natural" can be used to express the contrast between the incipient and the accomplished, for these words are clearly related by etymology.

Whether we use related words or one and the same word to express the beginning and the end, skill will be needed in handling such a necessarily and normally ambiguous notion as that of nature. If skill is accompanied by honesty and soundness, the task will still be hard enough. If skill is accompanied by diseased emotions and, say, qualified honesty, then we have Rousseau and his followers. One cannot be sure that Rousseau is always truthful; he sometimes is, like most men. That he is emotionally diseased is public knowledge because he has confessed it all. Now the *Discourse on the Origins of Inequality Among Men* (1755), the *Social Contract* (1762), and other expressions of Rousseauistic thought—whether by the hand of Rousseau or that of his followers—evidence the continual lumping together of two things, viz., what is natural to man as being most just, most adequate to his nature, and what is natural as most native, most primitive. The great example here is the life of hypothetical good savages in primeval forests such as travellers described it after they had read the writings of the philosophers on the natural goodness of man.

NECESSITY AND CONTINGENCY

Another theoretical subject of major relevance for the treatment of natural law is that of necessity and contingency. There is an urgent need for the clarification of these concepts. In the current stories about determinism and finality the word "determinism" implies a host of unclarified postulates which would, perhaps, be respectable if they were disengaged and formulated, but which are truly obnoxious so long as they remain mere gossip that has been running over the campuses of quite a few schools in the world for a number of generations. When we use such a word as "determinism," the most harmful illusion is that it conveys an unmistakable meaning. In most cases "determinism" is associated with a mechanistic vision of the world. This association is historically strong, but it is not doctrinally necessary. In Leibnitz, for instance, there is a theory of determination by sufficient reason [13] which (theory) is foreign to mechanism, although mechanistic explanations play a large part in his philosophy. "Determinism" is also generally associated with a monistic interpretation of the physical universe. If there were only one cause at work in this world, there would be no independent causal lines and no possibility of interference. We are back to the problem of unity versus plurality that Aristotle discussed against the Eleatics. When this problem is stated in terms of causal relations, it becomes particularly clear that the pluralistic answer is inescapable. A seed of corn will develop into an adult plant if the soil is good, if there is enough moisture, if it is not eaten up by a bird right away, if its young root is not destroyed by a worm, if the young plant is not swept away by torrential rain, if it does not serve as food for deer, and so forth. Nobody would believe us if we assumed that corn, soil, atmospheric circumstances, birds, worms, and deer do not constitute a real plurality of causes. We all assume that there are several causes at work in the world; but if they are several, they can interfere with each other, and a contingent event takes place at the point of interference. Whereas a seed of corn tends to develop into an adult plant, a hungry bird tends to develop into a well-fed bird, and the latter development may interfere with the former. If the plurality of causes and their interference are real, contingency is equally real, and the part it plays in the world, both physical and moral, may be huge. Indeed, some major philosophic systems exclude contingency by denying plurality or so restricting it as to make it harmless. The universe of the Stoics is *one* thing, and the Stoic Providence is there to make sure, in spite of appearances, that nothing fortuitous ever happens. We have mentioned the important part played by the Stoics in the development of ideas on natural law; let us never forget that any Stoic theory of natural law belongs to a philosophy which asserts universal necessity, and in order to be sure that contingency is ruled out, upholds the improbable representation of a universe endowed with the unity of an individual organism.[14]

Another philosophy which leaves no room for contingency is that of Spinoza. Here, as well as in Stoicism, we have to do with a system which is ultimately shaped by its moral purposes. Beginners are tempted to think that the title of Spinoza's most important work, the *Ethics*, is a misnomer, for the book so entitled contains a large amount of metaphysics. An illustrious mathematician once said that Spinoza "was perhaps in good faith" when he declared that he would treat all sorts of philosophical topics according to the method of the geometricians.[15] Whether Spinoza does or does not reason, in fact, in the geometrical way becomes an issue of secondary importance when we have understood that both his allegedly geometrical method and his metaphysics are directed toward definite answers to the problems of human life, of joy and pain, of worry and of peace of mind, and above all, to the problem of the freedom of man in the presence of death.[16] The philosophy of Spinoza becomes rather clear when one understands that all its parts converge on a theory of what the attitude of the wise man should be toward death, toward impending calamities, toward pain. Contingency has to be excluded from such a philosophy because Spinozian peace and joy are the sentiments that the wise and free man, as understood by Spinoza, comes to experience by becoming aware of universal necessity and of how insane it is to rebel and be resentful.[17]

It has been commonly held, for several generations, that the ill-defined things called science, or modern science, or modern philosophy, or rationalism imply a deterministic vision of the world and rule out contingency. But a new position is now playing a noisy role in the dialogue; it reminds us all the time that physics gave up the principle of universal determination about thirty years ago. The thing that is generally left unclear is this: what precisely constitutes the determinism negated by the prefix "in" when we speak of indeterminism in modern physics? The celebrated Louis de Broglie, generally considered the founder of wave mechanics, was among the first to declare that classical deterministic patterns no longer worked; but in a paper published in 1953, he spoke of a possible return to determinism.[18] In these and related controversies, the worst mistake would be to take for granted the meaning of such words as certainty, contingency, necessity, determinism, indeterminism, indeterminacy. Each of these words may convey diverse meanings and diversities of meaning that are directly relevant for the theory of natural law. No natural law would be conceivable in a world of all-embracing indeterminacy, in a world from which all determinate natures would be excluded; this seems to be the way things are represented by at least the most extreme forms of existentialism. Is it possible to speak of natural law in a system where Parmenidian unity obtains? Possibly, but the meaning of the expression "natural law" must be widely different, in a Parmenidian universe, from what it is in a philosophy which, by recognizing a plurality of determinate natures, makes allowance from the beginning for interferences, combinations and substitutions of forms, aggregates devoid of essential unity, and all sorts of accidents, whose frequency cannot be deduced from any principle and has to be learned by experience. These are matters where philosophic understanding is commonly slowed down by the unspoken agreement that basic problems of meaning will not be raised. At this price philosophers and scientists are sure that they can keep arguing, but what they are arguing about we are not so sure.[19]

FREE CHOICE

Throughout the history of philosophy there has existed a tendency to hold that a free act, if there is such a thing, is an event without a cause, an exception to the principle of causality. At the time when the indeterministic crisis broke out there were jokes—though not everybody meant them to be jokes—about "distinguished electrons" to whom ("to whom," not "to which") a certain freedom of choice should be granted. Whether free choice has anything to do with indeterminacy, with the principle of uncertainty such as it is understood by contemporary physicists (when they are working in physics), is quite a problem. The significant fact is that as soon as people hear that the principle of causality admits of exceptions, they begin to dream of new possibilities being opened to the old claim that man is a free agent. There seems to be in the human mind an everlasting readiness to associate free choice with indeterminacy and, under favorable circumstances, to place the principle of freedom in a lack of determination, in the lack of a positive feature, in a lack of causality and rationality. To exemplify our remarks on the relation between dialectic and the history of thought, we mentioned, in the first chapter, the Epicurean theory of freedom. It is truly a typical position which deserves always to be represented in the dialogue of the philosophers. The philosophy of Epicurus, still more definitely than that of Spinoza, is an ethical system. One main purpose of Epicurus and his followers is to liberate man from the fear of death, from the fear of the gods, and from the fear of fate. The atomistic physics of Democritus works wonders when the question is to remove the fear of death. If everything is made of atoms, if the soul is nothing else than an aggregate of atoms that are more polished and move more smoothly than others—as swiftly as thought—then death is no longer frightening. When it comes, the body disintegrates and so does the soul, which is but a part of the body. The fear of the gods is taken care of by the theory that the gods do not bother about human affairs. Being perfectly happy, why should they? One difficulty remains: it is the fear of fate. The physical philosophy of Democritus is definitely necessitarian, and Epicurus said that he would still prefer the whims popularly attributed to the gods to the necessity of the natural philosophers.[20] With the proper rites one may hope to placate the gods, but the necessity of the natural philosophers cannot be pacified. So the necessitarianism of Democritus had to be eliminated and replaced by a theory of nature which would be able to deal with the fear of fate. The *swerve* is found in the physics of Epicurus and not in Democritus. Democritean atoms move in a vortex ruled by mechanical necessity. According to Epicurus, atoms fall like rain but also have the property of deviating from the vertical. This property helps to explain the constitution of aggregates, but most of all it is designed to rule out the inescapable necessity asserted by Democritus' philosophy. The swerve of the atom is the principle of free choice in Epicureanism.[21] Do not try to account for the swerve itself: it is purely and simply causeless. It is immensely more divorced from causality than the chance occurrence of Aristotle, which does not have *a* cause but has several causes, which has no essential cause, but has several accidental causes. (*Phys.* 2.5.196b; *Met.* 6.3.1027b.) The swerve is causeless and irrational. Again, it constitutes an ever-lasting pattern for the philosophies which conceive free choice as an act without a cause. Concerning the worth of these philosophies, the least that can be said is that they involve postulates which ought to be disengaged, clarified, and examined. Some discrimination should be exercised before assuming that a free act has to be an event without a cause, an event without law and without reason, a thing akin to chance but more causeless than a chance event. If the opposite of this interpretation is true, if free choice is to be described not as a case of indetermination but rather as a case of superdetermination, as a distinguished case of domination over diverse ways of acting and over the diversity of acting and nonacting, the notion of a law immanent in free natures assumes a sense widely different from whatever its sense might be in a theory which conceives of freedom after a pattern of indeterminacy.[22]

REASON VERSUS WILL

When a so-called scholastic writer asks "whether the true is logically prior to the good" or "whether the intellect or the will is the higher power," ignoramuses indulge in clichés about the unrealistic subtlety of scholastic questions, their complete uselessness, and the obsolete character of the "old faculty psychology." Elementary acquaintance with the history of ideas is all we need to recognize the nonsense of these clichés for what it is. As remarked in the preceding chapter, there is no scholastic doctrine, but there is a scholastic system of problems. Whether primacy belongs to the intellect or the will is a good scholastic question, and the characteristic dispositions of the scholastic period demand that problems of this kind be plainly stated; this does honor to the period. The question of primacy between reason and will is as present and active among modern as among medieval thinkers, but when it is less clearly stated it is likely to be more troublesome. (In most, if not all, phases of its adventurous history, the notion of natural law is violently attacked whenever the voluntaristic trend is predominant.) The problem actually begins with the interpretation of positive law. When we are told that "this is the law of the land," we may be satisfied with the practical signification of these words and conclude that we have to conform or risk trouble. But if we care to go beyond such a behavioristic notion of conduct, we have to determine whether, by the law of the land, we primarily mean a rule worked out rationally, which always should be entirely reasonable and which falls short of its nature insofar as it fails to achieve complete reasonableness, or an act which holds because it is born of sovereign will and which, in order to hold, needs no other grounds than the sheer fact that it has been elicited by a sovereign will. The question is whether by the law of the land, we primarily mean a work of public reason or an act of will elicited by the sovereign (whether king or people makes little difference).

Legal voluntarism, i.e., the theory that law is primarily an act of sovereign will and, at the limit, an arbitrary decree of an absolute, unenlightened, irrational will, is historically associated in a remarkably constant fashion with voluntarism as a general philosophic position, i.e., with the theory that primacy belongs not to the true but to the good and that the higher faculty is not the intellect but the will. The limit of legal voluntarism was reached by the nominalists of the fourteenth century (Occam, 1300-1349; Pierre d'Ailly, 1350-1420) who, as we saw, held that God could order man to hate him, and that if such were the case, hating God would be meritorious. In more recent times, legal voluntarism is represented most outspokenly by Hobbes (1588-1679) and in a more qualified way by Bodin (1530-1596), a theorist of absolute monarchy, and by Rousseau (1712-1778), a theorist of the people's will.

The connection of the problem of natural law with the problem of God is perhaps more commonly acknowledged in our time than in any other period. The readers of Jean-Paul Sartre, who also have read Dostoevsky would despise as inconsistent, timid, and perhaps hypocritical the philosophy expressed in the famous words of Grotius, *etiamsi daremus non esse Deum.** There is no question of denying the connection between the problem of natural law and the problem of God. But it is not easy to show precisely what this connection is. One may wonder whether the study of moral nature and of natural law is a way to the knowledge of God or whether the knowledge of God must be had before the proposition that there exists a natural law of the moral world is established. We may be able to show that the truth is better expressed by the first part of this alternative.[23] Just as the consideration of beauty in things perishable leads to unparticipated Beauty—remember the speech of Socrates in the *Symposium*—so the consideration of law in human affairs leads to the unparticipated Law, the eternal law which is identical with the divine intellect and the divine substance. Acquaintance with natural law, being a way to God, would be logically antecedent to the knowledge of God's existence. But from this logical priority in the order of discovery it does not follow that the understanding of natural law can be logically preserved in case of failure to recognize in God the ultimate foundation of all laws. Again, the intelligence of natural law is a way to God.

---

* "What we have just said [about law] would still hold even if we granted that there is no God or that He is not concerned with human affairs." *De jure belli ac pacis*, Proleg., 11.

This means, for one thing, that it normally leads to the knowledge of God's existence and it means, for another, that if the way to God is blocked, no matter what the obstacle, the intelligence of natural law is itself impaired (this is logically inevitable). The latter seems to be the case in the atheistic forms of existentialism: the postulate that there is no God being given a character of fundamental premise, any proposition which would lead to its rejection is logically unacceptable; there cannot be a natural law because, if there were such a thing, one would be led to assert the existence of God contrary to a fundamental premise of the system.

* * *

Let us recognize that the question of natural law is itself philosophical. Further, it is related in the most inescapable way to profound issues of theoretical philosophy. Thus, the difficulties proper to philosophy are inescapably present in any discussion involving natural law. From this it follows that whenever there is a good reason to avoid these difficulties, there will also be a good reason to leave natural law out of the picture, whether by denying that it exists or by acting as if its existence did not matter.

In the present connection, the difficulties "proper to philosophy" pertain principally or mostly to the problem of communication, community in assent, consensus. Let the fundamentals of this issue be briefly stated. Wherever there is demonstration there is an absolutely firm ground for unanimous assent. An axiomatic proposition is necessarily assented to by any mind that understands it, and a demonstrated proposition necessitates the assent of any mind that considers it under the power of the demonstrating premises. But in this world of contingent occurrences there is an indeterminate discrepancy between the really normal and the factual, between that which would happen if essential necessities had their own way and what happens factually.* The popular belief—shared by a great variety of philosophical thinkers— that a genuinely demonstrated proposition necessarily entails factual consensus, and that failure to cause consensus is perfect evidence of failure to attain demonstrativeness, ignores the unpleasant fact that contingency affects intellectual life as certainly as it does the growth of plants in our forests and in our cultivated fields. There are departments of knowledge where demonstration, no matter how flawless, is unlikely to entail factual agreement except within small circles of kindred minds. Such is the case with all philosophic sciences, and if a man feels that he has no calling for solitary research, solitary contemplation, and solitary struggle against error, he should conclude that he has no calling for philosophy. But there are disciplines which by reason of their social function, and also by reason of the conditions to which their existence and their development are subjected, systematically seek factual communicability and the largest possible amount of agreement. Such is the case of all techniques (e.g., engineering, medicine) and of all the sciences insofar as they are directly or indirectly, proximately or remotely, dominated by technical purposes. Considering, further, that scientific research in our society is to an unprecedented extent the work of teams, it becomes clear that the successful communication of propositions is not only a condition of technical fertility: it is also a condition of progress and existence of such disciplines.

Another domain where factual agreement is sought sys-

---

* Assent to an axiomatic proposition is necessary as soon as this proposition is understood. Whether it is easy or not to understand axiomatic propositions is a totally different issue. The notion of logical immediacy, which means nothing else than the connection of a subject and a predicate without the offices of any intermediary term, must not be confused with the psychological disposition commonly expressed by the exclamations "That is obvious!"

tematically is that of positive law. There is no need to elaborate on this point: by the very fact that formulas of positive law are designed to hold men together, organize their cooperation, bring about uniformity in the behavior of indefinitely many individuals, it is highly desirable that these formulas should command the assent of all persons concerned or most of them. We must, accordingly, expect the jurists to evidence an eagerness to keep away from issues on which minds are irretrievably divided. In this respect there is a striking analogy between the case of the jurist and that of the natural scientist. Duhem, among others, said that if physics claimed to be an explanation of nature, it would soon become as controversial as metaphysics. Why should that be avoided? Again, because of the function that physics has to play in society and because of the social conditions of its existence and development. All natural scientists, no matter how divided they may be on the philosophic interpretation of their own science, would agree that the search for factual consensus plays a considerable role in their choice of questions and in the determination of their standpoints and their ways of research and expression. Thus the merits of consensus prompt the scientist to *abstract from* many aspects of reality which, indeed, may well be worth considering, which perhaps should be considered by somebody—e.g., by philosophers—but which have to be left out of the picture by men who absolutely need to understand each other in order to be able to work together. The same need for abstraction is felt in positive law. The ideal of the positive jurist, especially in societies deeply divided on philosophic, moral, social, and religious subjects, is a system of legal formulas which would be equally acceptable to the nominalist and the realist, the mechanist and the hylomorphist, the believer in universal necessity and the believer in the reality of contingency, the upholder and the denier of free choice, the rationalist and the voluntarist, the theist and the atheist. Is such a system possible at all? The least that can be said is that it would be low in intelligibility and would defeat a major purpose of the jurist, which is to explain the law. Jurists are caught in an antinomy: inasmuch as they are concerned with explanation they are inclined toward philosophical analysis, and they move away from desirable consensus; but inasmuch as they systematically seek consensus they are bound to abstract from the really illuminating issues which are philosophic and on which, as a matter of fact (though not by essential necessity), minds will always be divided. Legal positivism is considered by many a valuable compromise. But it is just another philosophy, and its being describable as the philosophy of the nonphilosophers does not give it power to win consensus. Yet the legal positivist may at least cherish the illusion that he is satisfying the conditions of unanimous assent; the theorist of natural law cannot cherish such an illusion. Accordingly, jurists generally favor some sort of positivism. The case had been different in the past, prior to the constitution of positivism as a distinct system of philosophy. But when the theory of natural law seems to be commonly accepted and works as a factor of agreement, there are good reasons to suspect that it is embodied in an *ideology*. Then the weight which brings about consensus is not that of objectivity; it is rather a sociological weight which is at best an embarrassing ally of truth. The conflict between the requirements of philosophic analysis and those of consensus may cause difficulties in the work of the philosophers; it inevitably causes trouble in the treatment of such a subject as natural law by jurists, for they, indeed, have strong reasons to seek consensus. And we cannot doubt that such problems will last as long as there remains any philosophic interest in nature and in law.

PART TWO

The Definition of Law / 4

THE INTRODUCTORY PART of this work being over, we now turn to the study of the concept of law. Order requires that we consider first the kind of law which is, and which in all events will remain, the closest and most familiar to us. The study of law begins with the consideration of what this word signifies when we speak of the laws of the civil society, when we say, for instance, "This is the law of the land." This order is determined by reasons of diverse character. For one thing, it is clear that the law of society comes before the law of nature in a psychological and pedagogical sense. For another, the analysis or resolution of man-made laws into their foundations is the very way to the position and determination of the question as to whether there exist laws of nature. Finally, even if there be such, we cannot yet presume that the concept of law applies in the same sense to the laws of society and to natural laws. The term law, as predicated of the laws of the state and the laws of nature, may convey not one meaning but a set of related meanings; briefly, it may be analogical.*

---

* In some cases, whatever member of the set comes after the first admits of no understanding except through the understanding of the first, and with

If this turns out to be the case, considering first the instance which comes first in the development of our cognitions would be more than a psychological and pedagogical convenience, and it would be more than a condition for determining whether natural laws exist; such order would pertain by logical necessity to the understanding of the concept of law as divided into man-made and natural.[1]

Let us, then, ask first how law should be defined in the case of the law established by human societies, by states. Now in the establishment of a definition, circumstances are most favorable when the term to be defined belongs to the language of daily life. Then the point of departure of our quest is clearly indicated: it is the commonly accepted meaning of the word, its nominal and dialectical definition. We call it "nominal" inasmuch as it expresses the distinction between the meaning of one name and that of another, and we call it "dialectical" inasmuch as it expresses an agreement among minds, a sort of a social settlement regarding the import of a word. From this starting point we may then work toward a strict definition. As to the objections to such procedure, the following should suffice. Aristotle raises (*Post. An.* 2.4ff.) the question whether a definition can be demonstrated, and his answer seems obscure to many readers. He seems to say that in a way it can and in another way it cannot. Absolutely speaking, the definition of a subject is that by which a certain

---

explicit reference to its definition (analogy of attribution and metaphorical analogy, e.g., "cheerful apartment" and "the ship plows the sea"; these "firsts" or primary analogates are, of course, the *cheerfulness* of the dwellers and/or of the interior decorator, and the literal *plowing* of the earth by the farm implement). When explicit reference to the definition of the first analogate is not needed, as in the analogy of proper proportionality (e.g., "good" as predicated of a physical condition and as predicated of a human action), the consideration of order among the members of the analogical set does not become irrelevant; the ground and the character of its necessity are among the most difficult and the least studied aspects of the logic of analogy.

property is demonstratively connected with this subject; a definition considered absolutely, i.e., in the capacity of definition, is antecedent to and presupposed by demonstration and this implies that definition is, as such, indemonstrable. But it happens that a term can be defined in more than one way, in which case an initial, more familiar, though less intrinsically intelligible definition may be used as the means to establish a better explained and more explanatory one. It remains true that definition is indemonstrable, for it is not as *definition* that the terminal definition is demonstrated; it is demonstrated as *terminal* definition entailed by an initial and provisional one.[2]

THE RATIONAL NATURE OF LAW

We find at the beginning of Thomas Aquinas' *Treatise on Laws* (*Sum. theol.* i-ii. 90.1) this nominal and dialectical definition of law: law is a rule and a measure of human action. Establishing the real and scientific definition will consist in determining what conditions a thing should satisfy in order that it be a rule and a measure of human action. The search for the real definition of law is subdivided into four questions, the first of which is whether law is a work of the reason.* The meaning of this question is made perfectly clear by referring (according to good historical and dialectical method) to the fact of legal voluntarism. What is not in dispute is that the legislator—whether king, representative assembly, or the people as a whole—wants a certain rule to be observed in certain circumstances. That every law involves an act of will is taken for granted. What is being asked is whether the role of the will in the constitution of the law is primary or subordinate. As remarked before, the history of voluntarism tes-

---

* The others are: (2) concerning the end of law; (3) its cause; (4) the promulgation of law.

tifies that this problem of order is not an irrelevant subtlety. Thus the first question in our progression from the nominal and dialectical to the real definition of law is whether, in order to have the character of a rule and a measure of human action, the thing called law should be primarily a work of the reason or a work of the will.

Of the terms involved in this question (rule, measure, human action, reason, will), none has the quality of intelligible ultimacy. Mathematicians—our teachers in rigorous thinking —are today more than ever particular about making their initial and indefinable concepts, as well as their initial and indemonstrable premises, entirely explicit. In philosophy, also, complete rigor requires that every concept be analyzed into its components up to the level of the indefinables. One reason why philosophy rarely exists in a perfectly rigorous and scientific condition is that the complete analysis of a philosophical term is an operation involving such strain that few people can stand it. A philosopher who cares to have any readers must generally stop short of the indefinables, just when he has reached a level where the reader experiences a feeling of sufficient clarity. If intellectual training is sound, this feeling is dependable, and if it is unsound, not much can be done anyway. Therefore, we shall confidently depend on the common understanding of such terms as "rule" and "measure." The latter term is somewhat unusual in the context of human affairs, but simple reference to its ordinary quantitative use suffices to make it clear, as well as graphic and effective, as a supplement to the term rule. If a thing is a rule and a measure of human action, what kind of thing is it supposed to be? Among the conditions that it ought to satisfy, shall we include its being primarily a work of the reason or its being primarily a work of the will?

Legal voluntarism is a widespread theory which does not often disclose its identity with complete bluntness. A few political thinkers of great renown are usually described as legal voluntarists, but one can easily gather evidence to the effect that neither Bodin, nor Hobbes, nor Rousseau fails to qualify his voluntaristic interpretation of law. Hobbes is perhaps the least inhibited of the three. Historians of ideas, especially when they are young scholars eager to write something novel on an old subject, often are inclined to emphasize the qualifications so strongly that the theory qualified seems to disappear: at this point the history of ideas becomes unintelligible. It is safe to assume that if the historic interpretation of a great political thinker has been what it has been, there are good reasons for its being such. Rousseau belongs to history as the philosopher for whom law is an act of the general will, an expression of what the people will, so that, in case of dispute about the justice or the wisdom of the law, the fact that the people wants it to be that way is final. No doubt, it is easy to abstract from the works of Rousseau a number of texts showing reverence for truth, rationality, reasonableness, and wisdom.[3] Such inquiries, designed to avoid abusive simplification in the interpretation of genius, ought to be performed; but when they have been carefully completed, the factual, the historical, the historic meaning of Rousseau remains to be accounted for and it is unlikely that it should be traced to mere accident. The *Social Contract* was not widely read before the French Revolution. Contrary to the ideological interpretation of history, so dear to persons who like to think that their party would never have been defeated if a vicious writer had not published a wicked book, it is not the *Social Contract* which made the French Revolution; rather, it was the French Revolution which promoted the *Social Contract*. But it is not by accident that the Revolutionists selected this, in preference to any other book, as the compendium of their philosophy. The political booklet of Rousseau, with all its subtleties, expresses powerfully the theory that the state is constituted by a total surrender of one's freedom to a general will with which one's own will is identified in a quasi-mystical way, so that, by obeying the will of the people alone one remains as free as in the state of native independence. This picture of identification of individual and general will supplied the emerging class with a powerful weapon in its fight against the institutions of privilege. The purpose of emancipation from the old bonds and the no less certain purpose of constructing a highly centralized and rational state were both served effectively by the ideology of the general will. A period of terrorism soon followed. To be sure, the scale of arbitrary executions was small in comparison with what we have been witnessing in this century. But one must remember that the sensibility of the late eighteenth century was not sheer hypocrisy. When the question was to vindicate the infliction of the death penalty on a few thousand persons, many of whom were plainly innocent, a really powerful excuse was needed. This excuse was procured, to a large extent, by the feeling that the general will—the one which is quasi-divine and with which the will of each individual is mystically identified—stood with the executioners. Danton once said that among those who ought to be put to death some were free from personal guilt. In the humanitarian atmosphere of the late eighteenth century, such decisions could not be proclaimed with such complete frankness, unless they were traced to a will which had the character of ultimate ground.* Indeed, Rousseau labored with subtlety

---

* In the line of Juvenal, *Hoc volo, sic jubeo sit pro ratione voluntas* (I will this, I order it, so let my will stand for reason [the fact that I will it is sufficient ground]), the word *ratio* seems to convey two related meanings. It designates the act of reasoning as opposed to the act of willing, and it designates "reason" in the sense of ground. An act of will is posited where an act of reason was expected (*sit pro*) and this act of will, by the very fact that it displaces an act of reason, takes on the character of ultimate ground. The striking power of this line, so often quoted to express the paradox of voluntarism, seems to be due to the lumping together of these meanings. The unity

on the general will, and what he finally had to offer was a confused idea. But all history testifies that confused ideas can be powerful. More than once revolutionists had found in Rousseau a burning vision of the peoples' will as the ultimate thing in civil affairs, and that was all they needed or cared for.

The proposition that "a thing which is a rule and a measure of human action is primarily the work of the reason" is axiomatic, and so we are again confronted by the particular difficulties that the handling of axioms involves in our time. Two factors should be considered. First, ever since the early ages of Greek culture men have looked up to mathematics for patterns of rigorous thought and held that if any propositions enjoy the power of absolute premises these should be the mathematical axioms. But in our time mathematicians commonly hold that no difference should be made between axioms and postulates. The so-called axiomatic proposition still plays the part of first premise but it is within a definite system that it plays such a part; in another system it would be a conclusion. Accordingly, the proposition *used as* first premise never has the character of an absolute premise. A day may come when the meaning of axioms in mathematics will be understood to involve unique particularities following upon the fundamental characteristics of mathematical abstraction. Then we may realize that looking up to mathematics for ideal patterns of axiomatic propositions was a precarious operation, jeopardized by illusions concerning the relation of mathematics to reality.[4] Although the theories of mathematics found in the works of Plato and of Aristotle probably contained all that was needed to rule out the belief that mathematics is the science of physical quantity, these illusions kept haunting the human mind down to the non-Euclidean revolution. And since the science

of the word *ratio* manifests the violence involved whenever the will, by assuming the primacy which belongs to the reason (*ratio*), also assumes the character of ground (*ratio*).

of mathematics reached a high state of perfection many generations before any other science had grown beyond initial endeavors, it was natural that patterns of rational thinking, with
regard to axioms as well as with regard to discourse, should be
looked for in mathematics. Again, the day may come when it
will be understood that, by virtue of the particular kind of
abstraction which distinguishes mathematical sciences from
any other ways of knowledge, mathematics is the domain
where axioms are just postulates and, consequently, the domain where archetypes of axiomatic expression should not be
looked for. But this day is far off, and in the meantime philosophers will have to struggle harder than ever if they want
to convince anybody that absolute premises, which the mathematicians say cannot be found in their own domain, can be
found elsewhere.

Secondly, the adventures of the theory of axioms in modern
times are traceable in part to the confusion of logical issues
with psychological issues. The sharp distinction to be made
between logical immediacy, i.e., independence of any middle
term and antecedent demonstration, and the psychological
situation designated when we say that we are ready to do something immediately, vanishes in any theory which fails to express the difference between psychology and logic. The psychological interpretation of logical properties has been a common
accident, especially since the seventeenth century. (One of the
reasons for the success of what is called "symbolic logic" is
that in this movement we find again, at long last, a sense for
something which, no matter what its nature may be, its certainly not reducible to psychological processes.) When Descartes proposed to substitute four simple rules for the countless
ones worked out by the logicians of the past, he did not replace a complex system of logic by a simple one, but a system
of logic by a system which is not one of logic. The four rules
of the method are not concerned with logical properties; they

are rules for the handling of psychological processes.[5] And if the rules for such handling can replace the rules of the logical art and the science of second intentions, it seems that logic is not only eliminated as superfluous and cumbersome, it apparently is rendered impossible. But over a period of many generations, and along various trends of thought, the real meaning of the Cartesian operation was not understood, and books principally concerned, in the Cartesian spirit, with the handling of certain psychological processes kept being passed off as treatises of logic.*

When we say that a proposition such as "a thing which is a rule and a measure of human action is primarily a work of the reason" is axiomatic, all that is meant is that if we understand the subject and the predicate of this proposition we also understand that they are to be connected by the copula "is." Their connection is intelligible without the help of a middle term, without the help of an antecedent demonstration. This is what "axiomatic" means,[6] and it implies nothing else; most importantly, it does not imply that the proposition which is immediate in a logical sense, i.e., independent of any logical intermediary between subject and predicate, is also accessible immediately in a psychological sense, i.e., readily understandable without preparation. In fact, the task of getting prepared to understand an axiomatic proposition may be difficult and long. It may take years or generations or centuries for the mind to understand a proposition that is logically immediate. The implication that if a proposition is logically immediate it should be readily grasped by all and bring about consensus

---

* When Professor Ferdinand Gonseth of Zurich describes the Logic of Port-Royal, a mixture of scholastic eclecticism and Cartesianism—all controlled by a sense for what is acceptable to lovers of belles-lettres—as an example of "Aristotelian logic," the only conclusion to be drawn is that a great mathematician and an honest and charming fellow may not know what he is talking about. See *Qu'est-ce que la logique?* (Paris: Herman, 1937).

is totally unwarranted. Such terms as rule, measure, human action, reason, and will convey deep subjects that cannot be analyzed without much hard work.

Human Action

Among these subjects let us concentrate on what is meant by the words "human action." Men do many things that are not considered human actions, and if we understand why these actions are not called human, we may have a chance to understand what kind of rule befits actions that are genuinely human. To scratch one's beard absentmindedly is not a human action. To talk in one's sleep is not a human action. To act by psychical constraint is not to elicit a human action. Why do we sometimes dismiss the case of a man who had killed his fellow human being? Lasting insanity, temporary insanity, and some emotional circumstances are reputed to deprive some actions of their human character. According to times and places, juries accept these considerations more readily or more reluctantly, but no matter how aware of the dangers of excessive leniency no tribunal would rule out the possibility that an act externally undistinguishable from the most horrible crime be just a natural disaster, a contingent occurrence in the course of natural events, an accident in the operation of cosmic energies. In such a case the act does not concern the administration of justice, except in so far as society ought to be protected against several kinds of diseased persons. When a man who seems to have acted under the compulsive power of pathological emotion is declared guilty by a court and punished accordingly, we all feel that an appalling injustice is committed. Suffering is inflicted upon a human being for an action which is not human; this is an extreme form of disorder.

Let it be noticed that a pathological emotion may leave a man free to resist or to yield. It is, first of all, by reason of its object that an emotion is describable as normal or as pathological. What suspends the human character of action, and causes a man no longer to be answerable for what he does, is not the object but rather the intensity of his emotion. Whether the object is normal or abnormal, an emotion impairs the human character of action when, and only when, its intensity renders it compulsive. Intensity, here, should be understood in relation to circumstances. An emotion which would have no significant consequences under conditions making for clear-sightedness and strong will power may attain compulsive intensity if a man's power to control himself has been weakened by fatigue, worry, physical disease, and other such factors. Concerning the relation between the abnormality of an emotion and its possible compulsiveness, it can be safely conjectured that when emotions are abnormally directed, ability to control oneself is also weakened. In other words, the factor which causes the misdirection of an emotion would also cause the weakening of the functions involved in self-control. But this cannot be more than a conjecture to be tested in every particular case. A man may be less able to control a normal emotion than an abnormal one.

How do we know that a case of killing is a cosmic event rather than a human action? We hold that the mind of a man is gone, that the use of his judgment is suspended, that his reason is out of commission. It is the presence of reason which makes all the difference. There is a cosmic event when a squirrel jumps from one branch of a tree to another branch, and there is a cosmic event when a completely insane person kills another person. A squirrel can be destroyed as a nuisance, but the insane man with a propensity to kill cannot be punished, although he should be restrained. Thus by reflecting upon the rational character of what is recognized as "human action" we come to understand that ruling human action primarily pertains to the reason. The rule of an action proceeding from the reason must itself be rational. If the will is reasonable, if it follows the reason, it is to the reason that primacy belongs; but if the will is held to enjoy primacy, it is also held to be free from reasonableness, from agreement with the reason, from direction by the reason. Such will is arbitrary, and the most adequate way to convey the rationality of the law may be to say that such a will is *lawless*. We would thus attribute to human action a condition that we would not dare attribute to natural processes. Indeed, no matter what the philosophers may fancy, all our behavior toward natural energies and all our understanding of nature testify that cosmic events are not lawless. A voluntaristic interpretation of law would place less rationality in human actions than in processes that are just natural. The absurdity of such an interpretation helps to perceive the truth of the opposite view and of its consequences. Human action, as compared with merely natural processes, demands a rule that is rational in character. A law is such a rule. Turning, then, to the problem of regularity in cosmic affairs we may one day come to understand that things also have their laws and discover reasons inside things.

At this point it is relevant to ask whether some human societies may conceivably be governed by rules of instinct and animal intelligence rather than by rules of reason. What is it that makes the difference between so-called animal intelligence and intelligence (or understanding, or reason) properly so called? The distinguishing characteristics of reason, as compared with animal intelligence, are most certainly attained by reflecting upon the profundity and the necessity that rational consideration involves in an indefinite multiplicity of ways. The pattern is supplied by abstract thinking, logical and mathematical. If Plato believed that the science of mathematics is such a distinguished teacher of mankind, it is, above all, because it develops in the mind a familiarity with rational necessity. Such absolute necessity is absent from any combination of images, no matter how subtle; it is also absent from the complex which associates anticipated pleasure or pain with a sensation or an image; and it is also absent from the sheer feeling that the thing attained in a particular experience or image is useful or harmful. This feeling is precisely what Aristotle calls the sagacity, the prudence, the wisdom found in animals—man not excluded—and which we designate as instinct and animal intelligence. (*Hist. Anim.* 8.1.588a20.) If we want to decide whether primitive societies, or some of them, establish their rules of action by animal intelligence rather than by rational consideration, let us bear in mind the character of necessity which distinguishes the rational. A legislative system which evidences a constant effort to embody a certain philosophy of man and society cannot be mistaken for a work of animal intelligence.[7] The rational character of the rules by which a society wants to be governed is more outspoken when the basic laws of the land are written in formal language, but it may be equally unmistakable when the principles of legislation are left unwritten and safely entrusted to enlightened traditions. Are there societies governed by totally unenlightened tradition and customs? Aristotle says that manual laborers act the way fire burns, inasmuch as their actions proceed from nonrational habit just as the action of fire proceeds from nonrational nature (*Met.* 1.1.981b2). Are there societies whose rules are as nonrational as the working habits of Aristotle's laborers? The answer pertains to sociological observation. The only thing that can philosophically be asserted is that if such societies exist they are subhuman, though made of human beings. Thomas Aquinas expressed the belief that the circumstances of climate may be such as to prevent the development of the reason in men. If such underprivileged men made up a society, their rules of common behavior would be infrarational. These hypotheses are not disproved by any philosophical principle but the modern study of primitive societies does not seem to bear them out.

The report accepted by Aquinas apparently was one of those amazing travellers' stories that our ancestors were so eager to believe.

Law and Practical Wisdom

Let us now ask in what capacity law is a work of reason and, more precisely, whether it is a work of reason in the capacity of conclusion or in that of premise. Sound method requires that we should consider first that which is ultimate in the system of practical reason, i.e., the fully determinate judgments which apply to action immediately. These judgments are as practical as the acts whose forms they are;[8] accordingly, they involve reference to all the contingencies of particular situations. The individual case with which practical judgment ultimately has to deal may always be in some significant respect unique, unprecedented, and unrenewable. Thus, the last conclusion of the practical discourse is marked in essential fashion by features of strict singularity and of contingency. These features contradict in several ways the already established characteristics of law. In fact, a practical judgment fully adjusted to the circumstances is not so much the work of the reason as that of an inclination. It cannot be connected logically with any first principle. It ought indeed to be connected with principles but, owing to the contingency of its matter, the soundness of an inclination is the only thing that can effect this connection. No necessity of discourse deals with data that are not contained in any rational necessity. At the level of practical ultimacy, "love takes over the function of object" and the determination of truth is the work of affective connaturality.[9] It is entirely reasonable that the last word about action be uttered by the inclination of the wise men, but there is less rationality in a judgment determined by sound inclination than in one determined by rational obviousness. Thus, considering this trait of law, viz., its being a work of the reason, let it be said that the conclusion of the practical discourse implies, in the most essential fashion, a trait opposed to the rational character of law. But more fundamentally, the last practical judgment, i.e., the one which is congruent to action as form is congruent to matter, is separated from law both by its singularity and by its contingency. A law is a rule and there is nothing more essential to it than the intelligible features implied in the concept of rule. These include universality and necessity. To be sure, both of these features admit of degrees: a rule can be more or less universal and more or less necessary. But in a judgment marked by singularity and contingency we recognize features opposite to those of law. Between law and action there always is a space to be filled by decisions which cannot be written into law. And the number of steps needed to connect the last word of the legislative reason and the ultimate form of action is itself determined by contingent particularities: it may be large.

Between the concept of authority and that of law there exist enlightening relations. It is, indeed, perfectly appropriate to speak of the authority of the legislator, and it would be arbitrary to identify authority and executive power. However, authority and law evidence opposite intelligible tendencies inasmuch as the more a proposition is expressive of necessity, the more it participates—other things being equal—in the character of law, whereas there is nothing in the concept of authority that expresses aversion to contingency. When authority serves to insure the united action of a community under circumstances which render unanimity precarious, authority is exercising an essential function. But after we have discounted all factors of a negative character, such as ignorance, shortsightedness, and selfishness, it is the contingency of our ways, the possibility of attaining our goal one way or the other, which renders unanimity precarious and causes authority to be the indispensable condition of steady unity in common action.[10] Authority is perfectly at home in the management of contingency and in the uttering of practical conclusions. Law is more at home in the realm of necessity. If any law is so grounded in a necessary state of affairs as to be unqualifiedly immutable, this is a law in the most excellent sense of the term. The expression "authoritarian government" may be considered redundant inasmuch as every government implies authority. Yet it is not by meaningless chance that this expression has come into existence, for in contrast to those governments which systematically proceed by law, as far as law can go, the governments which want their initiative to be, as far as possible, free from direction and restriction by law can be called authoritarian with some propriety.

Accordingly, the principle of government by law is held in check by the inevitable and fully normal contingency of the situations that government has to deal with. The significance of this principle is clear, for law admits of powerful and lasting guarantees against arbitrariness. Beyond the last settlement of law, man is but precariously protected against the arbitrariness of his decisions. A wise polity entrusts as little as possible to the good judgment of executive agents, but what it has to entrust to these agents, under penalty of destroying much human substance by doing violence to the works of history, may still be considerable. Government by law is a principle that must be asserted with special firmness and frequently recalled, precisely because it is inevitably restricted by opposite requirements. The principle of government by law is subject to such precarious conditions that, if it were not constantly reasserted, it soon would be destroyed by the opposite and complementary principle, viz., that of adequacy to contingent, changing, and unique circumstances.

*　*　*

If law is a premise rather than a conclusion, if, universally, law admits of no immediate contact with the world of action, the ideal of a social science which would, in each particular case, procure a rational solution and render governmental prudence unnecessary is thoroughly deceptive. Whatever the science of man and of society has to say remains at an indeterminate distance from the world of action, and this distance can be traversed only by the obscure methods of prudence which involve, in the most essential manner, the power of sound inclinations. This does not mean that social science is incapable of influence on the course of events and should remain dedicated to understanding and explanation.[11] Rather, the practical role of social science has to be exercised through the works of a wisdom which is not scientific. Prudence, practical wisdom, admits of a variety of states. In whatever state it exists, it remains a disciple of love. But it may be more or less enlightened. The more enlightened its condition, the better it satisfies the requirement that human actions be ruled and measured by reason. The practical task of social science is to give prudence access to a more enlightened condition. Thus the progress of social science is well in line with the requirements of prudence, whose duty it is to extend, in the obscurities of contingency, the work of the reason down to immediate contact with the world of action. But in order to fulfill this task, social science must give up the fantastic ambition it harbors of bringing about by its own power the rational society.

The consideration that a law is a work of reason in the capacity of premise raises the following problem in regard to the constitution of every legislative system. "Premise" admits of being understood relatively, in government as well as in theoretical science. A proposition acting as a premise in relation to further propositions is not necessarily axiomatic, it may be derived from antecedent propositions. That every legislative system contains many propositions derived from antecedent premises is obvious. The relevant question concerns the nature of this derivation. Are these derived legal formulas determined by logical connection with axioms, or are some of them the work of prudential determination? The answer is plain: indefinitely many legal formulas are the work of a legislative prudence and their determination has been worked out by the sensible, the dependable inclinations of experienced and well-intentioned persons. The obscure methods of prudence, which are at work in the space between the last legal expression and the ultimate form of action, are already at work, on a very large scale, within the system of legislation itself. This fact reminds us that laws participate unequally in the character of law. Inasmuch as a law is a work of the reason, the ways of inclination used by prudence, no matter how reasonable and necessary they may be, satisfy the essential implications of law less completely, less plainly, than the ways of rational necessity. A law is more or less of a law according as it has more or less completely and directly the character of a work of the reason. A privilege attaches to whatever aspects of the legal system bear the mark of rational necessity.

THE COMMON GOOD

Not every rule of human action is a law. We may speak with entire propriety of the rules that we wish to observe in our own lives or in the government of our families. Occasionally, we may call these rules laws, but there is something metaphorical about such a way of speaking. We do not even use the word law to designate a regulation—an ordinance—issued by city or county authorities. But we speak of state and of federal laws. In actual signification, then, "law" stands for a rule relative to the common good, and more precisely, to the common good of a community distinguished by amplitude and completeness.* The rules of such communities are spontaneously treated as being rules and measures of human action in an excellent sense. To ask whether this understanding of law is warranted is the same as to ask whether the common good has primacy over the private good. Indeed, there are rules in reference to all sorts of private affairs, but it is also taken for granted that the rule of the civil community, called law, is something superior which should inspire dedication, reverence, and awe. If it is ever lawful to act at variance with the law, it is by reason of some accident, such as ungenuineness on the part of the law or extraordinary circumstances. Some would like to believe that law can never be ungenuine, and that no circumstance can ever suspend its efficacy. Between these and their opponents, the discussion is about the range of accident; they are agreed that the law as such is final. But this implies that the common good of the civil society is, in some way, final and supreme. Is law, then, essentially relative to the common good? The answer will consist in determining whether the common good (best exemplified by the good of the most complete society) enjoys primacy over the particular good (best exemplified by the good of the individual).

This difficult subject may be approached by considering the diverse ways in which men expect to transcend the finiteness of their existence. Belief in the immortality of the soul, whether on a rational basis or on the basis of revelation, leaves problems of duration unsolved so far as the present life is con-

---

* It is hardly necessary to say that the idea of completeness, in the present context, is affected by relativity. To define the state by the character of completeness is not to imply that any human society can ever be complete absolutely speaking; the most complete human society remains incomplete in many respects.

cerned.* In this life, contemplation, joy, and the happier forms of love raise men above the world of becoming and destruction. But these true images of eternity are accessible, here below, only by rare privilege, and their supratemporal way of existing is quickly suspended by the needs of a life which never ceases to be engaged in the stream of universal becoming.

Men also derive much energy, in their relation to the destructive power of time, from hope for survival in new generations. And yet, there is something ambiguous about the immortality of the species. If the species is considered in the state of abstraction from individuals, it is affected by a logical condition which rules out unqualified existence; or, if it is considered as capable or unqualified existence, it is identified with the perishable individual.

The last method is the dedication of our effort to the common good. Societies do die, whether as an effect of internal causes or by destruction from without; in both cases, however, death is accidental. There is nothing in the nature of society that calls for its termination. Every community is virtually immortal. To serve the common good, to communicate with society in such a way that society comes to live within our

---

* As an example of what is meant here by "problems of duration," let us think of the management of an estate when death is in sight. Such problems hardly arise in the mind of a young man who, for most practical purposes, expects that he and his people will enjoy, say, a cherished home, during indefinitely many years. The question of what to do with a house assumes a new and more truthful meaning when age or disease make it plain that the enjoyment of this earthly home will not last for more than a few units of borrowed time. Questions of great social significance are involved regarding the things that the present owner is about to leave forever. Should they be sold or retained, should additional wealth be invested in their repair or improvement, etc.? The immortality of the soul does not, by itself, solve any of these problems. Neither does it solve problems of duration pertaining to goods interior to man, e.g., science, experience, and virtue, insofar as these goods pertain to the present life.

precarious existence just as we live in its virtual immortality is a method of overcoming death which is accessible to all men at all times. The only exceptions are the slaves, the outlaws, and the exiles: all these are known to be refused the natural conditions of happiness in life and in death.*

Thus, duration is a trait by which the primacy of the common over the private good is clearly established. But, more profoundly, it is completeness which determines the greater excellence of the common good. The most versatile of men suffer serious limitations and, just as certainly as the least gifted ones, they have to accept specialization as a condition of proficiency. In order that men should enjoy the most indispensable benefits of a division of social labor a multitude of laborers is needed. Against the popular myth which represents community life as essentially concerned with such so-called material goods as safety from aggression, shelter, food, or transportation and hospitalization, it is easy to see that the association of more or less specialized laborers is at least as necessary in the things of culture and noble life as it is in things pertaining to biological survival. Indeed, we would rather fight our way alone in a jungle than be without the help of the community in our access to scientific truth, or to the intelligence of beauty, or to the refinements of enlightened conscience. All these examples are relative to needs, whether biological, intellectual, cultural, or moral, but let us remove the pernicious and all too frequent illusion that the tendency of men to form communities proceeds exclusively from need, poverty, lacks, and wants of every description. Some forms of sociability do proceed, from our not having, all by ourselves,

---

* What we call the second method is considered here only insofar as it is distinct from the third. In fact, the man who derives fortitude, in life and death, from the hope of surviving in his descendants generally views his family, present and future, as a community, and it is by the continued existence and excellence of this community that he hopes to conquer death.

the things that we must have if we are to survive and to live well. But other forms of sociability, perhaps less conspicuous but not less profound, proceed from our accomplishments, our fulfillments, our plenitude, from the abundance and super-abundance of successful life. There is such a thing as disinterested sociability. And since divine love alone can be absolutely disinterested in all respects, there is such a thing as a need to give, a need to be generous, a need to act disinterestedly. This need is so deeply rooted in our rational nature that when it is frustrated it soon breeds a singular power of destruction.[12]

These fundamentals concerning human sociability ought to be borne in mind in order that the common good be safely distinguished from its counterfeits and from the substitutes which make it possible, at least seemingly, to do without it in individualistic philosophies. "The greatest good of the greatest number," in the language of the utilitarians, is such a substitute excluding the common good by the premises of the system. No doubt, a substitute is better than nothing, and men have laid down their lives for a common good which was inadequately represented in their minds by "the greatest good of the greatest number." To bring forth the qualitative difference between the common and the private good, let us remark that a good is common if, and only if, it is of such nature as to call for common pursuit and common enjoyment. It is not an addition, or a multiplication, but an objective relation of the thing desirable to the powers of desire and attainment which distinguishes the common from the private good. Public safety is an aspect of the common good, for it certainly is a thing which by nature has to be pursued by common effort and, if obtained, is enjoyed in common. The same holds for the training of characters by the irresistible power of state coercion, and the same holds for the treasures of knowledge available in our schools and our libraries. (A beginner mathematician, today, can easily do things which would have been immensely difficult for Archimedes or Descartes.) Above all, it holds for the constant action, silent most of the time, by which society maintains in each of us some clarity of moral conscience, some willingness to prefer the right to the wrong, and some comforting energy against the forces of desperation. When the structures of society break down, as they sometimes do in periods of critical changes, in revolutions and in wars, ordinary people soon yield to hideous crime. Then it becomes appallingly clear that whatever moral conscience can be expected to exist in large numbers of men, whatever decency, whatever resistance to perversion or to desperation can be expected of them, are goods of such nature as to be pursued in common and procured by the distinct causality which belongs to a multitude unified, differentiated, and stabilized in its differentiated unity.* It may be difficult to say in what respects man is, and in what respects he is not, a part of the community. What is not open to doubt is that insofar as the individual has the character of a part, the principle of the primacy of the whole signifies not only that the common good is greater, but also that the private good may have to be sacrificed to the greater good of the community. Remarkably, these views command a large amount of consensus so long as they remain unformulated. It is generally agreed that members of the police or of the armed forces or of the fire department are sometimes under strict obligation to expose themselves to probable, or almost certain, or humanly certain death in the service of the community. Disagreements begin when such principles as that of the primacy of the common good

---

* The case of ordinary people is described here because it is particularly clear. This does not mean that men of distinguished morality owe less to society, for their indebtedness is probably greater. But because they do not go plundering as soon as the police department becomes inactive, their case is not so obvious.

are formulated. As it often happens in human affairs, formulating fundamental and familiar truths involves, here, very great difficulties, and may occasion a variety of misinterpretations.

Counterfeit Common Good

Of these misinterpretations, the most frequent and the most confusing is epitomized in what we would like to call *the myth of a common good external to man*. The history of political science and, more importantly, the psychology of political leaders show how great the temptation is to conceive a human community after the pattern of a work of art and the excellent condition of the human community after the pattern of perfection supplied by a masterwork. In all domains of art, whether relative to beauty or not, there is perfection if the thing worked out is perfect, and the good of man is completely irrelevant. Gauguin probably would not have produced his admirable paintings if he had not deserted his family: his desertion was bad for his people and for himself but did not affect the quality of his painting. If a work of art is the accomplice of evil, so that whoever enjoys it is inclined to such human evils as disorderly passion or self-destruction, it may mean that the work of art ought to be kept away from men, but it does not mean that it is not a good work of art.[13]

Why is it that both men of action and political thinkers prove so tempted to treat the community of men as a work of art, that is, as a thing external to man? No doubt, an adequate answer to this question would comprise several instructive considerations. One thing at least is clear: the joy of the artist is not indifferent to the matter out of which the work of art is made. And a matter more noble than ivory, marble, and gold is man. Further, the joy of having realized a form of art, an idea that does not express pre-existent data but springs from the innermost life of the artist as creator, is increased when the matter is difficult to manage. The difficulties overcome give greater intensity to the feeling of masterly creativeness. When the matter is not only the most noble of all but also opposes to the schemes of the artist the unique difficulties resulting from intelligence and from freedom, when the matter of art is made of agents capable of the infinite, the joy of success in the handling of such a matter is one of the most intense that man can experience in this world. And just as the most modest teachers of history derive a sense of exaltation from a secret identification with the heroes whose prowess they narrate to school boys, so political thinkers, even though they may not be men of action in any sense, derive enthusiasm from identification with the molders of cities and states.

The illusion of the community of men represented as a work of art is powerful; to destroy it several approaches may be needed. First of all, the theory that political ability is a virtue and is not an art must be immediately supplemented by the consideration that several arts—indefinitely many arts—are the normal instruments of political prudence. Their role is instrumental indeed but instrumental does not mean unimportant. The genius of a musician may be frustrated by the poor condition of his instrument; the same can happen to a man possessed of political wisdom if the instruments that his wisdom needs are wanting. As examples, think of the importance of oratory, of diplomatic manners, of expertness in financial practice, of acquaintance with many sorts of technical possibilities in the life of a statesman. It is neither necessary nor possible that these and other arts and specializations be possessed, in a high degree of excellence, by the statesman himself; but unless he has some acquaintance, no matter how rudimentary, with these instruments of political prudence, he cannot communicate with the experts placed under him and direct them in their instrumental capacity. It is hardly necessary to say that the volume and the weight of all the arts instrumental to politics have much increased in modern times, so that the temptation may be greater today than ever to mistake the conspicuous system of these arts for the essence of politics. This illusion loses much of its power when we realize that the instrumental role of several arts in politics is fully normal, that their role may be of extreme importance without ceasing to be merely instrumental, that a great amount of human energy may be most normally engaged in purely instrumental functions, and that it may take some intellectual effort to understand a voluminous and conspicuous instrument for what it is. (In most churches and auditoriums of the world, the organist attracts less attention than the organ.)

Secondly, it should be recalled that no art solves any problem of human use. One may possess an art excellently and remain idle. And it is always possible to make a humanly good or a humanly wrong use of whatever art one masters, whether excellently or in a rudimentary condition. Moreover, the master of an art may use his mastery against the very purposes of his art if he pleases to do so; in the example of Aristotle, a grammarian may use his knowledge of grammar to make grammatical mistakes, if that is what he likes to do. A clever physician known to be possessed of criminal dispositions is the least desirable person at the bedside of a patient, especially if the patient happens to be an obstacle to the physician's designs. If politics were an art, a virtue would still be needed to decide what use should be made of it, but this prudence is politics itself.[14] Many people, more or less confusedly, reason along the following line: politics demands such and such an action, which unfortunately is criminal; we must oppose this action on ethical grounds, in spite of its being politically desirable. In this widespread interpretation of the case, the statesman is a technician indeed, but his power of decision is not final; final decision concerning the affairs of the state belongs to moralists. But either these are possessed of political prudence and of the power to enforce its determinations, and then they are statesmen in unqualified fashion (the role of technicians being only instrumental), or they do not have political prudence, and we end with the absurdity of a state where the ultimate power of decision belongs to moralists who are no statesmen.

The myth which identifies the common good with the perfection of a work of art and thus represents it as something nonhuman is constantly strengthened by the assumption that society, or at least the temporal, as distinct from the spiritual society, is concerned only with external actions, such as digging, orderly conduct in the street, marching, charging and retreating according to orders, paying taxes, fulfilling contracts, etc. Political society, in this view, would have nothing to do with what goes on in the heart of men. To ascertain the worth of this current opinion, we must consider the kind of reality that social and political life is made of.

As social sciences tried to profit by the experimental method which was so successful in the knowledge of nature, the notion of *social fact* acquired a central importance. What facts are social in a proper sense? To what types are the main social facts reducible? The most obvious example of social fact is constituted by the cooperation of men engaged in a transitive action of such nature as to require the unified effort of a multitude. The digging of a canal, the clearing of a jungle, the building of a railroad, the reclamation of swamp land, all are clear examples of social facts, and the good condition of such facts, the successful cooperation of men in the performance of collective transitive actions is an aspect of the common good. But when men are aware of their unity in knowing and loving or hating, we speak with entire propriety of their communing in acts of cognition and love or hatred. Here are immanent actions which, because of the awareness of unity, assume a social character.[15] Clearly, these communions are the most genuine and the most profound of all social facts, and the good condition of these communions, the good condition of whatever pertains to acting together in these immanent actions, is the deepest and the most precious part of the common good. We may imagine isolated prisoners watching the same play at the same time, each on a particular screen, without any awareness of what goes on in the other cells, without even knowing whether other cells are occupied. There is nothing social about the unity in the enjoyment of the play by these isolated spectators. Suppose now that the doors of the prison are opened. The men are free, with no restriction of their craving for community life. (Every community is in some way or other what Aristotle says of the state, a community of the free.) Should they happen to watch a performance together, we would recognize the familiar picture of communion in interest, in terror or pity, in expectation and suspense, in admiration and enthusiasm which also makes up the social significance of Greek tragedies, football games, and bullfights as well. With their experience in confinement and freedom, in isolation and community, these fellows would be exceptionally qualified witnesses about the true nature of the common good. By listening to the words springing from the abundance of their hearts we would come to realize quite clearly that the most important part of community life takes place in the heart of man.

This will be confirmed (and at the same time we shall understand that the common good is principally a good of use, a moral good, not a good of nature) by considering the case —paradoxical indeed but not unreal—in which a community has to choose between survival in infamy and righteous death. The arguments point to the relation between politics and morality. We have already noted the following position: in case of conflict between what is politically necessary and what is ethically right, politics must yield to ethics. (Again, this implies that the city is ultimately governed not by the virtue of the statesman but by that of a moralist, who will piously be listened to by the statesman.) Suppose that a community which finds itself at the mercy of a powerful invader is given a choice between extermination and such a felony as universal apostasy. The thing *politically* good would seem to be survival regardless of the cost, for the simple reason that extermination puts an end to the very existence of the community. But their duty would be to accept martyrdom. This argument begs the question. The contention is that what is politically good is not of moral nature, so that conflict can arise beween the politically and the ethically good, just as it frequently arises between the requirements of art and those of moral life. Thus granted that the common good of the political community is a good of nature, politics requires that the city be kept existent, and annihilation cannot be preferred except on grounds foreign to politics. Likewise, if one chooses to expose himself to certain death for a worthy cause, it will be on grounds foreign to any art conversant with the maintenance of individual life. But the hypothesis is arbitrary, as can be understood by considering the communions in immanent action which make up the principal, the most final part of political life. To commune in the act of choosing extermination rather than felony would be a climax of excellence in community life just as the fully voluntary acceptance of death in the service of a worthy cause is, for a person, the supreme act of righteous love.

Individualism

Individualism, i.e., the philosophy according to which the common good is merely a useful one, in other words, is a mere means to the good of individuals, often derives energy from the misinterpretation of what is, in fact, an essential and most significant feature of the genuine common good precisely considered as residing in men. A thing which has the appearance of a common good, inasmuch as it cannot be realized without common desire and common action, is not a genuine common good and may amount to sheer destruction if it is kept apart from the persons who make up the community. Because society does not exist except in individuals (connected by definite relations), the good of society demands, by nature and not by accident, a constant distribution to individuals.* The accomplishments of common desire and effort if left undistributed are actually kept out of society and denied the character of common good. To whom are they good in this unnatural state of separation? Not to the men assembled and not to the community which exists in them and nowhere else. They have been, in some way or other, appropriated by the men in power, and from common they have violently become private—an accident characteristic of corruption in community life. What causes the never-ending difficulty of the problem is that, on the one hand, goods cease to be common if they are kept apart from society and, on the other hand, common goods are destroyed if they are inordinately distributed. It is easy to think of many examples. In a celebrated passage of the *Communist Manifesto*, Marx and Engels declare that the bourgeoisie "has accomplished wonders far surpassing Egyptian pyramids, Roman aqueducts, and

---

* The distribution of which we speak concerns individuals ultimately but it may directly concern communities that are part of the distributing community. These two aspects of the subject should always balance each other: on the one hand, the parts directly concerned with the distribution of the common good may, themselves, be communities (this against the Rousseauistic pattern of a state which, ideally, would have but individuals under it); on the other hand, by the law that society—whether large or small and whatever its nature may be—exists only in ordered individuals, the part ultimately concerned always is the individual man.

Gothic cathedrals." So long as it remains in operation, an aqueduct very certainly belongs to the common good of the society which uses it. The constant delivery of water to homes and fields satisfies in particularly obvious fashion the law of distribution which is that of the common good. To imagine an aqueduct that would not be a part of the common good, we have to bring in such accidental circumstances as a deal between politicians and contractors for the building of an aqueduct where it is not really needed, absurd management which would leave the crops without water during the rainless weeks, extreme carelessness in repair, etc. Still more improbable circumstances would have to be brought in should we imagine a Gothic cathedral kept out of the community. On the contrary, it may seriously be doubted that the Pyramids ever existed within the community of the Egyptian people. What distribution of services ever corresponded to the immense amount of human labor engaged in the building of the Egyptian wonders? These seem to have served principally, if not exclusively, the ambitions of a few rulers. The Pyramids of Egypt are a rather clear example of an undistributed and undistributable common achievement. In most cases the results of common effort escape distribution and leak out of society in more subtle and inconspicuous ways. It does not happen so often that a despot uses an immense amount of collective effort to realize what is no more than a private fancy. In most cases the common achievement that will be distributed and the common achievement that will not combine in complexes so obscure as to give the corrupt leaders a large amount of safety. It does not often happen that an aqueduct is kept out of public service, but it often happens that a road is built, at great public expense, for the service of very few people, or that a public building is planned larger and more luxurious than public service requires; the difference between fact and need represents the part of the common achievement which is, and will remain, undistributed. Or think of treasurable properties such as rare works of art or books purchased at great expense of public funds. Easy regulations concerning their use would soon cause destruction; accordingly, access to rooms containing artistic or historic treasures ought to be strictly controlled, and those things cannot be loaned without strong guarantees. But if regulations are exceedingly strict, so that only very few persons can enjoy the treasures acquired by common effort, again, what should be *common* good ceases to be such: it is kept out of the community by failure to achieve proper distribution.

The difficulty which gives power to individualism now can be clearly stated: from the law of distribution embodied in the essence of the common good, does it follow that the common good has merely the character of a useful good, of a way leading to the end which would be the good of the individual? Let us try to outline an orderly discussion of this issue. We need, in the first place, definite ideas about what the notions of means and end actually imply. The means, as such, is a thing desirable that has no desirability of its own; if it is desirable at all, it is by reason of its relation to a thing possessing a desirability of its own. Then, let it be recalled that, whereas the notion of end, considered in itself, signifies terminality, the thing which is an end in one respect may also be a means in another respect. The notion of intermediary end is antinomic indeed, and hard to manage on account of its antinomic character, but it is not contradictory; a genuine end may not be a final one. Let it also be remarked that an end may be final in a genuine sense and yet be contained within an order which is not, itself, final.

If only we keep these specifications in mind, it becomes easier to realize that the law of distribution which is that of the common good in no way prevents the common good from enjoying the character of an end, and of an end higher than the private good, and of a final end if the community under consideration has the character of a complete community. The proposition that the common good is "greater and more divine" (Aristotle *Ethics* 1.2.1094b7.) than the private good, by reason of completeness and of duration, does not assume all its meaning until we have understood that the law of distribution pertains to the essence of the common good. Both in terms of completeness and of duration, the common good enjoys excellence because it is distributable to many. Again, if the thing which bears the appearance of a common good is forcibly undistributed, it loses its excellence but it also loses the character of community.

The notion of *order* which is needed to understand in what sense an end is ultimate is explained in this well-known passage of Pascal (*Pensées*, Modern Library, Frag. 792):

The infinite distance between body and mind is a symbol of the infinitely more infinite distance between mind and charity; for charity is supernatural.

All the glory of greatness has no lustre for people who are in search of understanding.

The greatness of clever men is invisible to kings, to the rich, to chiefs, and to all the worldly great.

The greatness of wisdom, which is nothing if not of God, is invisible to the carnal-minded and to the clever. These are three orders differing in kind.

Great geniuses have their power, their glory, their greatness, their victory, their lustre, and have no need of worldly greatness, with which they are not in keeping. They are seen, not by the eye, but by the mind; this is sufficient.

The saints have their power, their glory, their victory, their lustre, and need no worldly or intellectual greatness, with which they have no affinity; for these neither add anything to them, nor take away anything from them. They are seen of God and the angels, and not of the body, nor of the curious mind. God is enough for them.

... All bodies, the firmament, the stars, the earth and its kingdoms, are not equal to the lowest mind; for mind knows all these and itself; and these bodies nothing.

All bodies together, and all minds together, and all their products, are not equal to the least feeling of charity. This is of an order infinitely more exalted.

From all bodies together, we cannot obtain one little thought; this is impossible, and of another order. From all bodies and minds, we cannot produce a feeling of true charity; this is impossible, and of another and supernatural order.

The language used here by Pascal conveys the questionable simplifications pertaining to the Cartesian dualism of body and mind but this is, in the present connection, unimportant. What is significant is that Pascal expresses, with his unique power of words, the great metaphysical and ethical truth that all good of a lower order falls short of any good of a higher order. "The good of grace in a single soul is greater than the good of nature in the whole universe" (*Sum. theol.* i-ii. 113, 9 ad 2). The primacy of the common good is essentially due to a character of completeness which comprises the demand for distribution described in the foregoing. This primacy holds only so long as the goods under comparison belong to one and the same order, for as Thomas Aquinas and Pascal say, any good of the higher order is greater than the totality of the good that the lower order admits of.

But many suspect that the good of the individual man, inasmuch as it is a moral good, surpasses all the goods that are society's. This belief is best expressed by the heroic determination of those who, rather than undergo the defilement of sin, would accept death for themselves and for their beloved ones and also accept the destruction of their community. Can the fatherland be served by a crime? Many believe that it can and, of those many, a few declare that they will not commit a crime anyway. Now, whether we are willing or not to accept the defilement of our souls for the service of the common good—through such methods as lie, calumny, mock-trial and assassination—it is postulated that the common good pertains to the order of nature, not to the order of morality. The question whether I can pursue the salvation of my soul by sinning is ruled out by the obvious contradiction that an answer in the affirmative would imply. But, the question whether the preservation or restoration of my health, or the prolongation of my life, can be pursued through sinful action is a perfectly meaningful one. There are many cases in which, in order to remain alive or to stay in good health, neglect of duty, betrayal, breach of promise, stealing, etc., are clearly indicated methods. And we are divided as to whether health and life are worthier or less worthy than justice. (The bad thing with the control of society by physicians is that many of them, as a result of professional bias, take it for granted that the "scientific" answer is the one that prolongs life. To most of them it does not even occur that this conception of the "scientific," as opposed to the "nonscientific," implies a whole philosophic system concerning the meaning of the good and the relations between nature and morality, a system at least as questionable as any of the philosophies whose endlessly controversial character is scornfully set in contrast to the reliability of "science.")

The question whether the common good is physical or moral, which is one with the question whether it can be served (legitimately or not) by morally wrong actions is discussed by William E. Channing in terms whose thought-provoking power is increased by an artful shift of meaning and by felicitous order in dialectical steps.

Suppose the Public Good to require that a number of members of a state, no matter how few, should perjure themselves, or should disclaim their faith in God and virtue. Would their right to follow conscience and God be annulled? Would they be bound to sin? Suppose a conqueror to menace a state with ruin, unless its members should insult their parents, and stain themselves with crimes at which nature revolts? Must the Public Good prevail over purity and our holiest affections? Do we not all feel, that there are higher goods than even the safety of the state? That there is a higher law than that of mightiest empires? That the idea of Rectitude is deeper in human nature than that of private or public interest? And that this is to bear sway over all private and public acts?

The supreme law of a state is not its safety, its power, its prosperity, its affluence, the flourishing state of agriculture, commerce, and the arts. These objects, constituting what is commonly called the Public Good, are, indeed, proposed, and ought to be proposed, in the constitution and administration of states. But there is a higher law, even Virtue, Rectitude, the Voice of Conscience, the Will of God. Justice is greater good than property, not greater in degree, but in kind. Universal benevolence is infinitely superior to prosperity. Religion, the love of God, is worth incomparably more than all his outward gifts. A community, to secure or aggrandize itself, must never forsake the Right, the Holy, the Just.[16]

There is a significant uncertainty in this page: Channing first accepts the postulate that the public good may require perjury or impiety. His contention is that, in such a conflict, the public good should yield to the demands of conscience, just as all the good of a lower order is held inferior to any good of a higher order. But in the same passage Channing already suggests that "the supreme law *of a state*" is not such as to enter into irreducible conflict with "Virtue, Rectitude, the

Voice of Conscience, the Will of God." On the next page he writes:

> In this discussion, I have used the phrase, Public or General Good, in its common acceptation, as signifying the safety and prosperity of a state. Why can it not be used in a larger sense? Why can it not be made to comprehend inward and moral, as well as outward good? And why cannot the former be understood to be incomparably the most important element of the public weal? Then, indeed, I should assent to the proposition, that the General Good is the supreme Law.[17]

Supreme, indeed, not absolutely speaking, for the order of charity, in the words of Pascal, is above all the perfections of nature; but supreme in an order that it would be most inappropriate to designate as physical, material, or external. The common good of the civil society, which comprises such means and instruments as roads and bridges, is principally made of good human use, of free choice used as it ought to be. In this order of moral perfection, which remains essentially natural and never should be confused with the order of charity (in the strictly theological sense which is that of Pascal), the common good exercises priority as a direct consequence of the priority of the whole over the parts. The end of the moral virtues resides in the common good of the temporal society. Of this common good it should not be said that it is the ultimate end absolutely speaking, for it is ultimate within an order which is not itself ultimate.

The difficulties touched upon in this section, which remain great in the best conceivable framework, are often turned into forces of sheer destruction by a certain bias of ontological imagination. Every problem relative to the meaning and the rank of the common good depends on the answer given to the question: in what way does society exist, in what way is society something real? Regarding this question, the least that can be said is that it deserves to be treated with elaborate instruments. It is not a question which admits of such rough treatment as might place the borderline of reality at some distance, one way or the other, from where it actually lies. It is easy to imagine society as a big and awe-inspiring thing external to men and whose excellence, again, would be that of a work of art. To such excellence some are and some are not willing to sacrifice their happiness and their life. The myth of a society external to men commonly provokes an answer which literally denies the reality of society. But in many cases it should be wondered whether what is denied is the real existence of a society projected, by an accident of ontological imagination, into a space external to man, to human perfection, and to the perfection of man's use of his free choice. Such an accident is clearly apparent in Laski's discussion of the rights of society:

> ... the surrender we make is a surrender not for the sake of the society regarded as something other than its members, but exactly and precisely for men and women whose totality is conveniently summarized in a collective and abstract noun. I do not understand how England, for instance, can have an end or purpose distinct from, or opposed to, the end or purpose of its citizens. We strive to do our duty to England for the sake of Englishmen; a duty to England separate from them, and in which they did not share, is surely inconceivable.[18]

The last words express with the forcefulness of common sense the idea that we have been trying to explain, viz., that the common good is immanent in men and, in all its aspects, calls for a constant distribution to the persons who make up society and in whom society exists. "A duty to England separate from them [i.e., the Englishmen] and in which they did not share, is surely inconceivable." It surely is. But when Laski equates "exactly and precisely," society and the "men and women whose totality is conveniently summarized in a collective and abstract noun," he merely shows that the nominalistic mind is as unable to grasp the reality of a community as it is unable to grasp the meaning of a universal nature.

* * *

Not every rule and measure of human action is called law; the term is reserved for the rules issued by the state, which is a community distinguished by duration and completeness. To what purpose are such rules established? The spontaneous answer designates the end of the laws of the state as "the good of the society," "general interest," "the common good." But the almost universal agreement on this issue faces the difficulties attending all formulation of fundamental truths, and it dissolves in misinterpretations of the common good which these difficulties occasion. We have discussed two overlapping views, as stubborn as they are erroneous. The first is the myth of a common good external to man and conceived after the pattern of a work of art. The tendency, here, is to restrict social facts to material accomplishments and, consequently, to absolve politics of moral responsibilities. The second is the position defended by various schools of individualism, that the common good is merely a useful one, that is, "the greatest good of the greatest number." Its principal difficulties involve confusion regarding orders of means and ends and, in some cases, the familiar problem of the universals. In contrast with these views, we have tried to show that the common good indeed enjoys primacy over the private good of the individual, when both are of the same order, but that at the same time the common good is internal to man and by its very nature requires continuous distribution among the members of society. As such it is the end of the laws of the state.

* * *

In this discussion, as in Part One, no exhaustive treatment of all relevant topics can be expected. We shall deal with the remaining components of the definition of law briefly. Recall that the first was its rational character, the second its relation to the common good. The third concerns its cause. The principle involved is that of proportion between purpose and cause. If the purpose of law is common, the cause also must be common. Thus, law is a rule of reason, relative to the common good which, on account of its relation to the common good, proceeds from the community. The relevant difficulties concern the variety of ways in which a rule may proceed from a community, as well as the variety of communities. The two obvious cases are the civil community and the family. Clearly, rules for the welfare of the family emanate from the family; but babies, while certainly included, do not make rules. Not so long ago the exposition of the case would have been simple, as it was taken for granted that the family community had one head, neither appointed nor elected but designated by nature, who made the rules. Perhaps this is still true, at least in some cases. Of course, it is assumed that everything is normal; if the man is incapacitated and the wife is a wise woman, she will take over. Also, there is no reason why an indefinite number of decisions should not be made by the wife or even by the growing children. But there are more decisive, final issues concerning the family where the power of decision is invested in a head who is designated not by election, not by appointment, not by heredity, but by nature. Now to whom does it pertain to issue rules in the civil community? To a person designated by nature? To a person designated by God? To persons designated by heredity? To persons designated by election? To the whole multitude? These are familiar questions. In their modern form, they were first formulated at the time of the Renaissance in the conflicts between church and state. If the king is the representative of the political society, why should not the Pope also be the representative of the church? Do the laws of the spiritual society emanate from the spiritual society the way the laws of the civil society emanate from the civil society? Those who wanted to curb the power of the Pope and assert the authority of the church as community over its head reasoned by analogy from the principles of the civil society. Is not the civil society, at least in a crisis, superior to its head whom, if he is unworthy, it may depose? So begun, the dispute continued through centuries gaining only in confusion. Let us merely recall that the use of the expressions "divine right" and "sovereignty of the people" is unwarranted unless the several and incompatible meanings of each of them are defined with the utmost care.[19] For our purposes, the third component of the definition of law has been gathered: the making of law belongs either to the community as a whole or to someone who is in charge of the community. The fourth and last component will not be elaborated in this context: law has to be promulgated, it has to be conveyed to the knowledge of those who are subject to the law. The full definition then reads: "Law is an ordinance of reason for the common good, promulgated by him who has the care of the community." (*Sum. theol.* i-ii. 90.4, trans. A. C. Pegis.)

Natural Law / 5

It is clear that "law" as predicated of the rational rule and measure of human action issued by the most complete community and "law" as predicated of the regularity in the phenomena observable in physical nature are analogical terms. The analogy involved is that of proper proportionality; it is not metaphorical analogy, and it is not analogy of attribution.[1] That is, the understanding of the proposition "this is the law of the land" does not depend on the understanding, say, of "the law of gravity," and the latter does not depend on familiarity, say, with the writ of *habeas corpus*. In both cases "law" is understood properly and proportionately to its context, as "good" is understood when predicated, for instance, of a mother and of ice cream. What about the "law of the moral world," the "natural law of morality"? Whether there is such a thing or not, its meaning is not completely reducible either through attribution or through metaphor to either the "law of the land" or the "law of gravity." Abstracting for a moment, from the question of its existence, it is clear that "natural moral law" has an independent meaning related to the "law of the state" and to the "law of physical nature" by analogy of proper proportionality. Now in a set of meanings connected by proper proportionality, it often happens that what comes first in our cognition comes second in intrinsic intelligibility, plenitude, and genuineness. But as soon as the first analogate in intrinsic intelligibility has been reached, albeit in most rudimentary fashion, the analogate first in our cognition is seen in a new light. Its own intelligibility, as a member of an analogical set, increases and, consequently, it becomes capable of leading to a still better understanding of the analogate which is first in intelligibility. Our thought accomplishes progress through a dialectical movement, as it were, back and forth from the first analogate in cognition to the first analogate in being and intelligibility and back again. Because any analogical set, in which the order of cognition is inverse to the order of nature and intrinsic intelligibility, is made of the multiple predication of an absolute perfection (e.g. "duration" as predicated of time and of eternity), metaphysical contemplation as a human activity itself situated in but mastering time, if it is to achieve the excellence that it admits of, paradoxically implies a never-ending movement. These considerations do not detract in the least from the demonstrative and scientific character of metaphysics.[2]

FROM POSITIVE LAW TO NATURAL LAW

Our method, then, is as follows: we start with the most familiar case and move from the better known to that which is less known in the same order of ideas. Considering first "the law of the land," which we shall from now on call simply positive law, we have arrived at a definition and have explained some of its components. The next step is to ask whether the understanding of the positive law leads rationally to an antecedent, to a more profound or universal law, which we might call the "law of nature." This question is best approached by three lesser ones, the first of which is, does it make sense to ask whether a positive law is just or unjust? Referring to received opinions that carry great weight, i.e., those held by all men or the majority, all experts or the most highly reputed of them, we find here a strange case of unanimity. Some professors of law, of course, would dissent but they could not be entirely consistent, for this would require that they not only express themselves but also behave as if it made no sense to ask whether a law is just or unjust. True, a law may be just or unjust in many ways. The law by reason of which we drive on the right side rather than on the left side of the road is not just exactly in the same way as the law which punishes assassination. Yet both seem just in some way, albeit for different reasons. The obligation to drive on the right side of the road cannot be considered unjust. Some might like it better to drive on the left side, but they would grant that it is essential that everybody drive on the same side. In Great Britain they drive on the left side, in the rest of the world on the right. This is so probably because the right hand is stronger than the left hand, because the structure of the human body inclines toward the right rather than toward the left. But it does not really matter. Even if it had been decided by tossing a coin, we would still be agreed that the law by which we are obliged to drive on the right side has never been unjust. Moreover, this law becomes a little more just every day as the habit and the tradition of driving on the right side become more ancient. In fact, if any legislature suddenly decided that we should all begin driving on the left side the day after tomorrow, that would be an unjust law. The example is hypothetical, but it shows how a thing initially indifferent is transformed under the weight of habit and tradition to such an extent that overthrowing it would constitute an injustice of the first magnitude. How many thousands would die in the first week of the new regime, if such a law were passed? Again, the justice of the law by which we drive on the right side is not of the same kind as the justice of the laws which prohibit murder, theft, forgery, counterfeit, etc., but in all cases asking whether a law is just or unjust makes sense. (Whether an unjust law should be obeyed is another, different, and posterior issue [*Sum. theol.*, i-ii. 96.4.]) The only exceptions to unanimity on this question would be a few professional legal positivists or some skeptical lawyers, but these exceptional attitudes are not held with consistency. Whether they are held with sincerity cannot be known. The most skeptical lawyers and the most cynical of professional legal positivists will be revolted by some laws; for instance, the laws of discrimination against non-Aryans in Nazi Europe. There is no legal positivist who has not repudiated them, unless he was himself engaged in the operations of the Nazi regime. On what ground? That they were iniquities, that they were unjust? Perhaps, for the sake of professional consistency, such words are avoided, but the meaning of the rejection is clear. No matter how strictly all the formalities are observed with regard to the established principles of a regime, the law by reason of which innocent children of innocent parents are taken away from their parents and both, parents and children, are killed —no matter how "positive," that law is unjust. The problem of injustice certainly exists with regard to every positive law.

Writ large, the question whether it makes sense to talk about the justice of positive laws extends to cover the entire political system. Pragmatists are at their worst when they contend that the vindication of democracy in terms of natural law is obsolete, ineffective, and uninteresting.[3] They seem to believe that it is much more effectively presented by the consideration that democracy "works." Now here is a familiar expression found in any number of papers and glibly expounded in departments of philosophy, departments of political science, and in schools of law. But what does that mean,

"Democracy is better justified pragmatically by the consideration that it works"? What does "it works" mean? It means something, it makes sense, if there is a set goal, an agreed end; working is the most obviously teleological thing in the world. For instance, the Salk vaccine works. This means we are all agreed that it is better for children, youngsters, and even middle-aged people not to get paralytic poliomyelitis than to get it. There are no exceptions, we are unanimous: it is desirable in all respects that this dreadful disease should make as few victims as possible, not one if possible at all. When we read that in 1957 there were about thirty cases of paralytic poliomyelitis in Chicago against over one thousand in 1956, thank God, it works. It works in two ways: it works technically, and it works humanly. Health is not the absolute end of man; to be good in the capacity of a healthy organism is not the same as to be good as a man. What Plato would say of a good shoemaker may be said of the organism in good health, namely, that it is not the human good but a thing good in a certain order. Nevertheless, considering the totality of the good of a person and, more definitely, the good of the community as a whole, clearly it is better that there be few or no victims of poliomyelitis rather than many or some. It is in relation to this defined purpose that a certain vaccine is said to work or not to work. In a completely different kind of example, suppose we are discussing the problem of juvenile and non-juvenile criminality in a city and inquiring into the diverse methods used by the police department. We would say that a certain method works and that another does not. That makes sense because we are all agreed in advance that it is better that our pocketbooks should not be stolen, that we should not be beaten, that women should be able to go out unaccompanied after six o'clock without fear of attack, etc. We are all agreed on all that and we can speak of working and not working because of that initial agreement on ends.

Without such initial setting of ends the notion of working is purely and simply nonsensical. We can see here how pragmatism is a philosophy which makes sense within some pre-determined limits. But that is no longer philosophy. It is a certain way of looking at things in terms of success, in terms of action, and that has always been done. The distinction of pragmatism is precisely to have expanded that attitude of all times into an all-embracing philosophy. Of course, they have not been able to do it consistently. To do so they would have to work out notions of working and not working without defining that which works and that which does not work in relation to a set end—an obviously impossible task.

The second question which leads from the understanding of positive law to the law of nature is put as follows: on what grounds does positive law happen to be changed? [4] In a sense, we have already discussed this question, since one answer may be that a law is being changed because it is unjust. Another explanation may be that the law does not work, for instance, because it is not enforced. But this implies that it is just, good, desirable that a certain legal formula be applied. It may be said further that the law should be changed because it does not work in any sense whatsoever: it has grown obsolete, it is no longer adjusted to circumstances. But this implies that finalities which are adequately served in a certain way under some circumstances should be served in another way under changed circumstances. Suppose, for example, dissatisfaction with a law protecting people against dishonest money dealers. One hears stories, once upon a while, about small banks or credit organizations which offer a return well above the going rate. On closer examination it is found that investing with such outfits involves risks and dangers against which naïve people are not sufficiently protected under the existing legal circumstances. The argument to change the law would be presented somewhat as follows: our legislation is obsolete;

it was satisfactory three generations ago, but in the meantime economic circumstances have changed, and forms of credit have developed which were not foreseen by the legislators at the time; this law is no longer adjusted, no longer adequate. "Adjustment," and "adequacy," are nice pragmatic terms but, of course, we are postulating that it is better that people should not be robbed than robbed of their savings. In fact, we would make absolutely no sense if it were not taken for granted that when people have earned money lawfully they have a right to keep it. If it is to be taken away from them it should be within the guarantees of law, by taxes, social security, etc., and not arbitrarily by unscrupulous money dealers.

The third question which leads from positive law to natural law is the famous one, why should law be obeyed? If there is no idea of an antecedent law, the reason why positive law should be obeyed is entirely contained in the constraints possessed by civil society. The law then becomes a hypothetical system which may be formulated as follows: if I want not to be thrown into jail, if I want not to be shot down on the spot, if I want not to be driven out of the country . . . , then I have to comply with the laws of the society where I live. But this intepretation is unanimously or all but unanimously rejected. Can the ground for obeying the law be reduced, completely and in all cases, to a desire to avoid the trouble which would follow if the law was disobeyed? No doubt, there are such situations, but the proposition does not hold completely and in all cases. A law levying a certain tax may be abusive in the opinion of many good citizens, and they may say that they are complying simply in order not to be thrown in jail. One speaks and one thinks that way in extreme cases. But such reasons, argumentations, and interpretation cannot be extended to all legal propositions in all respects. To do so would void positive law of all obligation and ground it in sheer power. Here, again, we find a consensus which weighs a great deal. There is an almost universal reluctance to interpret the obligation to obey positive law in terms which annihilate it and replace it by a system of physical constraints where there is no choice, no freedom, and no morality.[5] The obligation to obey positive law obviously requires a different interpretation and this must be derived from the definition of positive law. We have proposed the following: law is a rule of the reason for the common good, promulgated by the community or by those in charge of the common interest. When the formula is such there exists an obligation to obey the law. Is that self-evident? It should be. But do not forget that self-evident does not mean perceptible without effort. A proposition is self-evident when the predicate adheres to the subject by reason of what these terms mean and without any logical intermediate. To perceive that immediate adherence we must be acquainted with the terms. In order to perceive the propositions "obeying genuine law is obligatory" in its full self-evidence, we must understand the definition of law as a rational premise relative to the common good, etc., and we must understand the notion of obligation. But such clarifications take time and despite perhaps considerable effort still remain unintelligible to some minds. In the meanwhile we have to rely on a grasp by inclination, which is never superfluous and which is sufficient so long as the rational grasp has not been achieved. Would you want to drive on the left side of the road if you were given firm guarantees that you would not be prosecuted for anything that might happen?

To sum up. No one could maintain with any appearance of consistency that it makes no sense to ask whether a law is just or unjust. And if we confess that the question makes sense, we also confess that there is a justice anterior to human enactment, that prior to their being just by reason of enactment some things are just by nature. These considerations also explain why a law happens to be changed. Finally, to say that law should be obeyed exclusively because of the trouble which somewhat regularly follows upon the breaking of law is dialectically impossible. Men have never reasoned that way. When a society is in such a condition that its laws are obeyed only insofar as there is real danger of being caught and punished, it has already disintegrated and even the fear of punishment cannot do much to hold it together.

THE DIVISIONS OF NATURAL LAW

The above reflections all suggest that *nothing would be right by enactment if some things were not right by nature.* Notice that the words of this proposition are carefully weighed. It does not say how many things are right by nature; it does not say that many are determined by nature as right or as wrong. The ratio of the right and wrong by nature to the total amount of the right and wrong is not under consideration. What matters is not whether many things are determinately right or determinately wrong by nature: *the relevant question is whether* some *are.* Even if we could speak of strict determination by nature of right and wrong only in extremely few cases, that would suffice, and that is all we are concerned with for the time being. Do the legal systems established by men demand that some things be, perhaps in a variety of ways, right or wrong by nature?

We need to consider the meanings of the word "right." The first refers to that which is right, the thing that is right, the objective right. For instance, we make a contract by reason of which the amount of money I owe you on the first day of March is one hundred dollars. The payment of one hundred dollars on March 1st is the right, the thing that is right, that is what it is supposed to be. That is the primary sense of the Latin *jus*, which is the root of a number of familiar words. Both doctrinally and historically this meaning may be treated as the primordial, although in legal, philosophical, and theological literature *jus* does not always have that sense. Aristotle uses the word τὸ δίκαιον, which would be the Latin *justum*, the just. If I give you only ninety-five dollars, when I owe you one hundred, the amount is five dollars short of being right. That is the objective sense of right.

The second meaning of "right" involves it with a law. That which is right is always such, in some way or other, by reason of a law. In fact, the law by reason of which what is objectively right as such is also called *jus* in Latin, *Recht* in German, *droit* in French, *diritto* in Italian, *derecho* in Spanish. In English it is called "law." This famous particularity of the English legal language has probably exercised considerable influence on the Anglo-Saxon way of thinking about juridical (or *legal*) matters. What is called the study of *jus*, *Recht*, *droit*, *diritto*, *derecho*, is not called the study of right in English, but the study of law. A whole library could be filled with controversies as to whether it is felicitous or not that one and the same word, "law," should be used to express the two ideas which are expressed in Latin by *jus* and *lex*, in German by *Recht* and *Gesetz*, in French by *droit* and *loi*, in Italian by *diritto* and *legge*, in Spanish by *derecho* and *ley*. These semantic problems, to use the word in fashion, are by no means uninteresting. But what remains of primary importance are the meanings and relations of meanings behind the terms. That which is right is such by reason of a law; reflect on the expression, "There ought to be a law!"

The third meaning conveyed by *jus*, *Recht*, *droit*, *diritto*, *derecho*, and by "right" is the legally recognized and sanctioned claim or faculty to do this or not to do that. You may not be arrested for speeding if you drive at thirty-seven miles an hour where the speed limit is forty-five miles. You may have an accident, you may kill somebody, you may be arrested and punished for a variety of mistakes, but not for speeding:

the law gives you the right to drive up to forty-five miles an hour. This notion of right as claim and faculty makes it reside in a person, or in a community, to whom something is due that may be described as a good, as a service, or as a freedom to do or not to do. Among the difficulties, doctrinal and historical, in the interpretation of the theory of natural law the primary sense of "right" is not the least one. But it is generally agreed that in the eighteenth century what was meant by "right" in English and by *droit* in French was, first of all, a claim, a faculty. The adoption of that meaning as primary was certainly an epoch-making event in the history of notions concerning law. Perhaps there had always been doctrinal and ideological trends in which the emphasis and the frequency belonged to this third meaning of "right"—right understood not as the thing which is right, not as that which is objectively right, but as that which one can claim as due to him by reason of contract, by reason of positive law, by reason of custom, or by reason of nature. At the end of the eighteenth century, in the American and the French Revolutions "right," no doubt, meant precisely that. And since then natural rights designate those claims to goods, to services, and most of all to freedoms that are due by nature.[6]

We return to the primary meaning of "right" in the sense of that which is right. The question is whether there are things which are right by nature. The right by nature, if there is such a thing, would be that which is right by reason of what the things are. In other words, if some things are right by nature, that implies that a law exists in the nature of things. Here we have to consider first the unity and then the contrast in the expressions "natural law" or "law of nature" as applied to the physical and as applied to the moral worlds. In the physical sciences the concept admits of a number of different interpretations, but one thing is certain: we cannot do either theoretically or practically without some notion of law. We may intepret it in the so-called causal terms or in statistical terms, according to the deterministic schemes of Newtonian physics or according to the indeterministic framework of the new physics born in the late 1920s (and whose destiny seems to be at stake again since the 1950s): what matters is the concept of law embodied in things. This concept not only makes sense but expresses a reality that absolutely nobody doubts. For instance, we all assume that sulphuric acid has a steady way of behaving which is definitely at variance with that of some things which outwardly look very much like it, say, sherry wine. Now it is not impossible that there be a container with sulphuric acid in a laboratory, and it is not impossible that in the same laboratory a glass of the same shape and size should contain sherry wine. But mistaking the former for the latter would be frightful in its consequences. Pragmatists are excellent on such matters: the two things behave quite differently; they produce distinct consequences. And it is agreed that *no drinks are served in laboratories.* Do you recognize here not only a discreet example of the general consensus on laws embodied in things but also an important aspect of unity between the physical and the moral worlds? Ever since the time of Kant (at the very latest) it has been the passion of several trends of more or less idealistic philosophies to sharpen the contrast between the universe of nature and the universe of morality.* And yet, the contrast is not so complete. Things have natures, and having natures they have within themselves laws of, let us say, operational behavior. But man, after all, also has a nature; man resembles other things inasmuch as he also has a nature. There is an interior, an immanent law of operation which connects the universe of mankind with the

---

* It is, of course, always possible to find forerunners of Kant, in the eighteenth century or even earlier. And the separation of the universe of nature and the universe of morality had been nicely prepared by Cartesian dualism, although it is dualism of another kind.

universe of physical nature. Indeed, laws of the physical kind extend to a number of aspects of man. There would be no psychology if this was not the case. Whatever may be said about the theory and practice of certain contemporary schools of psychology, psychology remains a useful natural science. Memory, for instance, is subject to laws which are very much like the laws of chemicals or the laws of plants. By reason of what it is it has a relatively uniform way of operating, and it is both theoretically and practically interesting to know more about this uniform way of operating. When we learn enough, we can devise techniques to improve memories and to preserve good memories. Then, the same can be done for emotions, though here the case is more particular because, obviously, we are closer to the world of free choice. But there are emotional determinations that are anterior to free choice. When persons with peculiar tendencies are examined they often reveal that their predispositions are contemporary with their earliest childhood recollections. Being antecedent to free choice, such inclinations clearly—in so far as these things can be ascertained—belong to the universe of nature. In case of obnoxious tendencies, sound moral advice may result in their repression, but it would be better still to eradicate them, to pull them out like bad teeth through appropriate techniques. These things are not completely impossible, and they belong properly to psychology.

What is particular about the natural law of man, of the moral world, is that essentially it operates through free choice. It exists as a rule inherent indeed in the nature of things but which does not direct operation in determinate fashion. It governs behavior through judgment and through free choice. This is best illustrated and explained by reference to the primary division of natural law according to Thomas Aquinas (*Sum. theol.*, i-ii 94.2). Thomas Aquinas shows that all natural laws are in some way contained in a most universal principle, viz., the principle that the good is to be pursued and the evil is to be avoided. This is *the* natural law, just as the principle of identity is *the* principle of reason. But just as the principle of identity is particularized in a hundred ways so natural law is particularized in many ways. The first division is as follows: there are in man tendencies which he has in common with all things, above all, the tendency to keep existing. That is not special to man, that is not special to animals, that is not special to living things; it is a universal property of being. In a completely different philosophic context, Spinoza proclaimed it in his famous words: "Every being strives to persevere in being." [7] Now here it can be seen clearly that suicide is something unnatural in the most radical sense. The conditions in which suicide is committed are certainly widely diverse. When we hear of a case, we are reasonably inclined to think that a crime has not been committed, that probably the person was out of his mind and did not act voluntarily. This does not mean that voluntary suicide is impossible. But it is reasonable, in case of doubt, to assume that it is not voluntary, because it is so obviously and so deeply contrary to nature. It is contrary to the universal inclination of being, which is something more profound than anything pertaining to the living or pertaining in strict appropriateness to man.

In the second division of natural law belong the inclinations that man has in common with animals. These involve especially the many and obscure matters pertaining and related to generation. Here man communes in a sense with all living nature, but more particularly with the animal nature, since both in man and in many animal species there is some infra-rational control of these inclinations. Included in this division are the matters of sex in general, the association of male and female, the care of offspring. For instance, all other things being equal, is it natural that mothers should take care of their own babies? Simone de Beauvoir once wrote a famous book called *The Second Sex*.[8] Among the reviews, that in the *Scientific American* made an excellent point. This journal is mostly dedicated to mathematical and physical sciences, but it regularly has a brief section for the so-called human or social sciences. The reviewer reported the author's remark that it was insane to entrust the care of babies and the upbringing of children in general, to creatures so bitter and frustrated and resentful as many mothers tend to be. Granted, wrote the reviewer, but to whom should the care of babies and the upbringing of children be entrusted? Who is less frustrated, less bitter, less resentful, less neurotic, and at the same time more loving, more dedicated than their own mothers? [9] Of course, there are mothers who are completely incompetent. But these are the kinds of problems that pertain to the second division of natural law dealing with inclinations proper to animal nature.

In the third division of natural law belong the inclinations proper to rational beings. There are innumerable problems which pertain to the right and the wrong by reason of what the rational nature is: requirements of life in society, the desire to know the truth, problems of obedience, problems of government. The natural inclinations under this third heading are proper to man as a rational agent. Thus everything that is right by nature is right either because the universal nature of being is such, or because the universal nature of animal is such, or because the rational nature is such. This threefold classification insures the community between the natural law of the moral world and the natural law of the physical world, no matter how sharply these laws may be contrasted in some respects. After all, man is part of this universe; after all, man has a nature.

No Kant scholar would insist that Kant denied this unity. But the most constant tendency of Kant and the Kantian tradition is to strengthen, bring forth, overdo, render overwhelming, if not theoretically exclusive, the contrast between the universe of nature and the universe of morality.[10] In truth, the great difference between the natural law of the moral world and the natural law of the physical world is that the physical world acts simply by nature, whereas man acts by nature, by animal nature and by rational nature. Sulphuric acid in contact with metal or with organic molecules acts by nature, according to its own nature. *You* would not put your finger in a glass containing sulphuric acid because you *know* that it will not change its mind and *you do not want* to lose your finger. The natural law of the moral world is immanent in a person by reason of his being a being, by reason of his being an animal, and by reason of his being a rational agent with inclinations, tendencies, aspirations which cannot be arbitrarily chosen. Concerning human behavior, either we are walking in our sleep and then we are not acting as human agents, or we are wide awake and then it is by judgment and by choice that we act either according to or at variance with the inclinations of being, the inclinations of the animal nature, and the inclinations of the rational nature.

ON THE KNOWLEDGE OF NATURAL LAW

Whatever language is used to express the last proposition above, few would deny its application in the daily life of individuals, of small groups, and even of large communities. In practice we all act as if there were a natural law with standards for measuring human behavior. In theory, however, some have trouble incorporating a natural law of mankind into an overall system. This is an interesting situation. Perhaps we can understand it better if we ask directly what is indeed a formidable question: how do we know the natural law of mankind? The physical world is left out of the picture. Henceforth natural law means what we understood it to mean from the beginning of this inquiry: the natural law of the moral world. How do we know it? That is the problem and it is not an easy one. Objections and difficulties with regard to the very statement of the question are great and must immediately be recognized. Among them the following is the best known: if there is such a thing as a natural right or things right by nature, this right or these things should be recognized by and known to everybody. Strange mores are observed in the Pacific islands, the Amazon jungle, the four corners of the world, and throughout the history of mankind. Moreover, even among ourselves some would judge a thing purely and simply good, while others would condemn it absolutely. Take, for instance, a subject like euthanasia. In our society one finds people having tea, playing bridge, and doing more important things together, being good friends. And yet some of them think that killing a patient who has incurable cancer is murder, while others say that it is a charitable thing to do. A man is gone anyway, he has no possibility of accomplishment or enjoyment; he is in this world for a few more weeks or months, with no other prospect but to stand terrible suffering; give him a pill of morphine and let that be the end of it for him and everybody around him; it is better that way. Now that is certainly a problem of natural law under the first heading above: should the inclination of being to keep existing be respected in the case of the miserable patient with no hope of recovering? Only a few more weeks or months of terrible suffering. . . . What is the right thing to do, right by nature? [11] Not only Greeks and Barbarians, Londoners and Fiji Islanders are divided on the issue; people belonging to the same circles in a rather homogeneous society also disagree. Clearly, the question, "How do we know natural law?" is not an easy one to answer or even to approach.

Here, what is needed is a digression of a sort—a strictly necessary digression—concerning two modes in the determination of judgment. Let us say two ways, it sounds better in the vernacular—two ways in the determination of judgment. They are the way of cognition and the way of inclination. Indispensable in all parts of ethics and in a few other branches of philosophical inquiry, this distinction is extremely familiar. I take a certain judgment, let us say, s is p, and I wonder how it is determined. Roughly, it may be determined by antecedent cognitions up to axioms or experience. The determination must end somewhere, and it ends in one way in axioms and in another way in experiences. That is what we try to do in rational science. We take a proposition on which we may be agreed or not (it does not matter, though it would be nicer if we were agreed). How do we establish this proposition? It is not self-evident, one cannot say that it is immediate; the predicate is not contained in the subject, and the subject is not contained in the predicate; so we are looking for a middle term. This may take a few centuries, but when we have found the middle term we have premises, and from the cognition of the truth of those premises follows the truth of the conclusion. That is rational knowledge and nothing is done in science, strictly speaking, so long as we have not done that. Of course, this is achieved fully, rigorously, perfectly only in very rare instances. In fact, what is called a science is made of a small nucleus, a hard core of really demonstrative knowledge, around which are built layers of fairly established and probable propositions and opinions. But the ideal of rational science is attained only when the proposition under consideration is established by way of antecedent cognition up to immediate axioms on the one hand and direct experiences on the other hand.

Now it would be very unfortunate if this were the only way of judgment—the way of cognition. It is perfectly clear, however, that many judgments are determined by way of inclination. To all kinds of propositions I say "yes" rather than "no," or "no" rather than "yes," as a result of an inclination. Is that arbitrary, a kind of wishful thinking? It certainly is if it is applied in domains where judgment by cognition is available and in all cases where wishes are not what they are supposed to be. But if the inclinations are sound, the judgment which is assented to because of agreement with an inclination is perfectly certain in its own way.[12] In fact, this is the only way to ascertain practical judgments when they are considered concretely. Examples are innumerable. Suppose you are in business, and a would-be partner has a project beneficial to you, to him, and even to the community at large. Now when business projects are so wonderful there is usually something wrong with them. But you cannot see anything wrong, the project appears perfect. The fellow is very smart, it is probably not for the first time that he is telling that story. So you do not see the "gimmick," but you can "smell" the fellow. Indeed, judgments by way of inclination are often expressed by this metaphor. "Are you going to make the deal?" "No." "And why not?" "Because the fellow, excuse me, stinks." There is an inclination in the honest conscience of a man trained in justice which makes him sensitive to the unjust even when he is completely unable to explain his judgment. In fact, such judgments are by their very nature incommunicable. That is why persons who have to help others with moral problems must acquire a number of moral signs and symbols. A man in charge of helping young people with moral problems cannot afford to say, "No, don't do that. I smell something rotten in the whole thing," and leave it at that. It is not enough, it does not suffice, because judgment by way of "smell," judgment by way of inclination is not communicable. A minimum of explanation is needed and must be provided. It is not to be hoped that it will ever be possible to demonstrate even every general rule of moral conduct, but some elucidation, some understanding, some connection with received principles is absolutely indispensable when there is direction of other persons because, once again, the judgment by inclination is, as such, incommunicable.[13] It can be held in common, but that is not the same thing. We can be twelve persons trained in justice in commercial practice, for instance, and receive an offer from a real crook who is smart enough not to show what is wrong with his scheme. And we may all twelve of us say "No." We do not need to explain to each other because we all have the same reaction, the same inclination to reject the offer.

When moral problems are considered concretely—in all their concreteness and individuality—the last word belongs always to sound inclination. There are no exceptions. There is always some aspect of the entirely concrete, circumstantiated issue—individual, unique, unprecedented, unrenewable—some aspect that can be decided only by inclination. There is a true theory that in case of extreme necessity I may help myself or help my baby with some food that does not belong to me. Yes, but who is going to decide whether or not I am in the condition of extreme necessity? That depends on and varies greatly with circumstances. In Wisconsin in September, if I were hungry, I would not have to feel terribly hungry to pick an ear of corn in the immensity of that field of corn. But in Greece in 1945-46, when all babies were short of milk, to take or not to take a bottle of milk belonging to someone else was a much harder problem for a mother. Only the inclination of the honest heart provides here the right answer. When moral problems are considered on the completely concrete, practical level, on the level of the last word, as it were, that last word belongs to inclination.

But law is a premise; it is a work of the reason having the character of premise. And among laws, the natural laws have more the character of premises than positive laws; they are prior premises. What has been said concerning ultimate conclusions in moral problems does not answer the questions concerning those premises, including the first premises which are called natural law. How are they known? By way of cognition or by way of inclination, or in both ways? One way is not necessarily exclusive of the other. There are cases in which a man spontaneously exclaims: "Oh, no. I won't do that. I don't do things like that!" He judges by way of inclination. Pressed for an explanation, the man ponders and finally says, "Yes, I can tell you why." And then we have a judgment by way of cognition. The explanation, the connection with antecedent cognitions is established. But the example again bears upon an ultimate practical conclusion. What about the premises themselves? What about natural law? Is it known by inclination? Is it known by way of cognition? Is it known both by way of inclination and by way of cognition?

It may be helpful, at this point, to recall something that happens quite often in the practice of all theoretical sciences. In the history of geometry, for instance, some theorems were formulated and firmly and universally accepted as true some time—perhaps a few centuries—before they were demonstrated. How were these propositions established that turned out to be demonstratively true centuries later? How were they formulated centuries earlier when there was no demonstration? By a kind of felicitous accident which happens to minds gifted and trained in the sciences. The better trained the mind, the more likely it is to come upon the true proposition by an inclination which, in this case, is not affective but purely intellectual. It is not the inclination of the heart of Professor X, it is inclination of the mathematical mind of Professor X that leads him to the true proposition. This happens in all the sciences, including philosophy. In their purely intellectual world progress often is achieved through movement from ascertainment by the inclination of the scientific mind to ascertainment by rational evidence. Something similar occurs in the case of natural law, though there is a very important difference: the inclination leading to the knowledge of natural law is not a purely intellectual affair. In science competent persons—especially competent persons—adhere to theorems proposed by experts even when there is as yet no demonstration. The intellect of the expert—that is why he is called an expert—is expected to conjecture, to guess the truth of scientific propositions. In the case of natural law the inclination involved, once again, is not purely intellectual. Here the inclination is that of the good, the honest will, and the expert is the prudent, the wise.[14]

In the works of Aristotle there are two passages on natural law. One is found in *Ethics* (5.7.1134b.) and the other in *Rhetoric* (1.13.1373b). Aristotle was not expansive on the subject, but what he had to say on it is worth studying. The passage in *Rhetoric* (trans. W. Rhys. Roberts) reads in part:

For there really is, as every one to some extent divines, a natural justice and injustice that is binding on all men, even on those who have no association or covenant with each other. It is this that Sophocles' Antigone clearly means when she says that the burial of Polyneices was a just act in spite of the prohibition: she means that it was just by nature.

> Not of to-day or yesterday it is,
> But lives eternal: none can date its birth.

The reference is to the famous page of *Antigone*. Antigone is blamed for having buried her brother against an order of the ruler of the city. Her brother was a rebel and was therefore to be denied the honor of a decent burial. But Antigone gave him this honor, and when challenged by the ruler, who was her own uncle, she explains to him that over and above the written laws there are some that are unwritten, that are eternal—

no one knows when they had been enacted. *Antigone* is justly recognized as one of the greatest documents in the history of natural law.

Aristotle maintains that "there really is, as everyone to some extent divines, a natural justice and injustice." "As everyone to some extent *divines*." "Divine" translates the verb which is related to mantic; the root is also found in a few compounds like geomantic, necromancy, cheiromantic and hydromancy. The dictionary gives the following meanings: to perceive through sympathy or intuition; to detect; to foretell; presage; portend; to have or feel a presage or foreboding; to conjecture or guess. No doubt Aristotle in this passage maintains that natural law is known by inclination. There is knowledge by inclination of what is naturally just and what is naturally unjust. Does knowledge by inclination exclude knowledge by rational evidence? Certainly not; it precedes it. Natural law is known by way of inclination before it is known by way of cognition.

Let us take a simple example. What do you think of cheating in the execution of a contract? Two men have signed a contract. It is explicit, and it binds one man to a certain difficult and costly performance. There was hard bargaining, but there was no duress. The contract is signed. But this man is still thinking of a way out, and he somehow manages not to execute that part of the contract which involves a heavy sacrifice for him. Now we all think that this is wrong. How do we know that? How do we know that it is wrong to cheat in the execution of a contract? No doubt, we all find it disgusting. We may be in disagreement on many issues, but we would all agree that it is perfectly disgusting to cheat in the execution of a contract in the signing of which all the normal circumstances are realized. The man bargained, he was not taken by surprise. He knew what he was doing. And knowing what he was doing, he cheated in the execution of a contract. We all find it disgusting. How do we know that? By an inclination? Certainly. The proposition is, "Let us cheat in the execution of this contract," and we feel a real repugnance. It is good that we should feel that way. Here is something unjust by nature, unright by nature. It is identified by way of inclination; or rather, the conflict of a certain rule of action with an inclination warns us that this is not right, that it is wrong. Wrong by reason of what? No doubt, by reason of nature. To be sure, it is by human enactment, by free choice that the contract was made; the situation is obviously man-made. And yet, we know by unmistakable inclination that it is wrong to cheat in the execution of a contract. We could say that that is clear, except that the word "clear" is ambiguous in this context. Knowledge by inclination is not clear; it may be certain, but it is not clear. In fact, it is incommunicable. It is perfectly sufficient for the fulfillment of an obligation, but it is not enough in order to understand. A virtuous inclination and a repugnance to do otherwise are sufficient for fulfillment, but one cannot teach an inclination or a repugnance. Rhetoric and example are ways of influencing people, but they do not amount to rational communication. Again, fulfillment without understanding is very often all we can do, but the nature of human fulfillment demands that there be a tendency toward as much understanding as possible. Not only from a theoretical point of view, which is obvious, but also from a practical point of view it is relevant to have as much understanding as possible, because human fulfillment must be as rational as possible. It matters from the very standpoint of fulfillment that there be understanding of what is being fulfilled.

Now notice that in our example the judgment is not merely one by inclination; it is also judgment by rational apprehension. The language of the contract is clear; there was bargaining and deliberation; the signing was free from duress. Anyone recognizes, therefore, the essence of the wrong in the proposition, "Let us cheat in the execution of this contract." The judgment, "Cheating in the execution of a contract is wrong," is known to be true both by inclination and by rational apprehension. One perceives, one apprehends, one recognizes the essence of the wrong in the subject "cheating in the execution of a contract." It is an immediate proposition. It is not only rational, it has a character of an absolute premise, which does not have to be demonstrated by an antecedent premise. The predicate is of the essence of the subject: "wrong" is of the essence of "cheating in the execution of a contract." The proposition is axiomatic.

A comparison with a purely theoretical case may again be helpful. Modern mathematics has made everything so postulational—"relative"—that there are not many cases left for an expression of strictly axiomatic thought. But we may be able to find at least one. Take the most skeptical, the most sarcastic, the most nihilistic of contemporary mathematicians and logicians. They all agree that from the true one can infer the true, and from the false one can infer the false, and from the false one can infer the true: the thing impossible is to infer the false from the true. Consider the relation between the proposition p and the proposition q. If p is true q can be true. If p is false q can be false. If p is false q can be true; one can by accident infer the true from the false. The thing that can never be done is to infer the false from the true. If p is true and if the inference is valid, then q is true by axiomatic necessity. Now, of course, certain mathematicians and logicians will not confess that they believe in axiomatic necessity, but they all keep assuming that if p is true and the inference valid, q is necessarily true.

In the proposition, "Cheating in the execution of a contract is wrong," the predicate is of the essence of the subject. There is no middle term, there is no demonstration. It may be used

as a premise to demonstrate some conclusions, but it is itself
not a conclusion in any sense. It is a formula of natural law.
And it is also a good example to show how formulas of natural
law admit of both ways of judgment; by inclination and by
cognition. The truly enlightening question is, which of the
two ways is antecedent? In case we are not yet completely clear
concerning a certain moral issue, which one of the two ways
of knowing can we expect first? The judgment by inclination,
of course. It is here the same as in the theoretical sciences,
with the important difference that, whereas in theoretical sciences the inclination is a purely intellectual affair, in matters
of natural law the inclination is appetitive or volitional. It is,
indeed, quite normal that we should distinguish the right from
the wrong by inclination before we are able to apprehend the
essence of the right or of the wrong in such and such a subject.
Psychoanalysis has given the word "rationalization" a bad
sense, but we may use it in this context in its extreme analyti-
cal meaning, namely, of grasping rationally that which so far
has been grasped indeed but not yet rationally. The rationalization of what has already been grasped by inclination is a perfectly normal aspect of our progress in the understanding of
natural law. There are domains of human action where rationalization so understood does not seem to involve excessive
difficulties. For instance, in matters of exchange the rule of
justice is awfully clear: an exchange is just if, and only if, the
values exchanged are equal. All the problem—not necessarily
always easy—is to ascertain their equality, and improvement in
the evaluation of things in exchange will normally advance our
apprehension of justice. But the field of justice in exchange is
rather simple. Its admitted difficulties appear quite manage-
able compared, for instance, with the problems of marriage,
sex, and related subjects, which are immensely more mysterious and refractory to rationalization. Consequently, in these
matters judgment by way of inclination assumes an almost

unique importance. An excellent negative example here is Bertrand Russell. In his writings on these subjects there is a total absence of inclinations and repugnances, rational or emotional. The only thing at work is the intellect, which in these matters can be extremely thin. Lord Russell has a great mind and he has written admirable things about a number of topics. But when he takes up the subject of marriage, sex, and morals, he tells all he knows, and he knows nothing. He is a good mathematician, an interesting logician, in some respects a considerable philosopher, and always a master writer. But when he writes on marriage, sex, and morals, he reveals not only his ignorance but also a considerable perversion of judgment. His writings illustrate convincingly what is left when judgment by inclination is completely gone, when there are no prepossessions left, when freedom from tradition is recklessly asserted. Then, what is left, in fact, is nothing, and the attempt to substitute something strictly rational for that nothing is a vain illusion.

ON OBLIGATION UNDER NATURAL LAW

We return to the problem of obligation. It was first mentioned briefly in connection with positive law, the clearest and the most familiar case of law. Recall that the notion of natural law was introduced by considering three questions. First, does it make sense to ask whether a law is just or not? Second, what is the ground for changing laws? And third, what is the meaning of obligation under law? Now some would say that they obey the laws of the state when they cannot do otherwise without considerable inconvenience to themselves, which reduces obligation to coercion or threat of coercion. This is not a very satisfactory explanation. The least that can be said is that it does not cover—or seem to cover—all the observable facts to which we refer when we speak of an obligation to obey a law.

We need to recall another point already discussed, namely, that before natural law exists in our minds as a proposition it exists in things. All other things being equal, we hold that it is better to live than to die, that it is better that mothers should take care of their babies rather than dispose of them, that it is better not to lie than to lie. This is so because of what these things *are:* because man is a being, because a mother is a mother, because human beings are rational agents. We express these natures rationally, and we have the first component of the definition of law: it is a work of the reason. But notice that it is a reason measured by things, which bows before things: that is what we mean when we say that those things are right by nature. The natural law exists in nature before it exists in our judgment, and it enjoys the latter existence—that is what natural law means!—by reason of what the nature of things is.

How do these rather obvious considerations connect with the problem of obligation? To explain the problem of obligation away by assuming that the feeling of obligation is reducible to fear of coercion is a rather arbitrary way of getting out of a profound difficulty. The depth of this difficulty is clearly seen when we once again point out that natural law, in the very meaning of that expression, exists ontologically before it exists rationally in our minds; it is embodied in things before it is thought out, thought through, understood, intelligently grasped. Plainly, it is *because* natural law is first embodied in things that we declare such and such an action to be right, and such and such an action to be wrong, under circumstances which may have to be defined with great attention and particularity. And here we find ourselves face to face with the real problem of obligation. It is clear what happens if we stop here. If we stop here, the last word does not belong to the reason, the last word does not belong to that which is intelligent. The last word belongs to things. That is the real problem of obligation.

We are told that we should all drive on the right side of the road, and we realize that this is a man-made regulation. But what is not a man-made regulation is that, if we are confronted with two possibilities, one leading to terrific manslaughter and the other avoiding manslaughter, it is by reason of what things are, by reason of what is naturally right, that we should do what avoids rather than what causes manslaughter. That is a formula of natural law. Now there is a further step, which is made not by way of logical connection but by way of prudential determination. We have to select the side on which everybody will drive. The right side was selected in most countries, the left side in Great Britain. This disposition is obviously man-made. But when such a man-made disposition is actually given effect, then it is by reason of what is naturally right that we must drive on the side selected. If we do not, we shall more than likely cause manslaughter and perhaps destroy ourselves, and that is wrong by nature, wrong by reason of what human beings are, by reason of what the physical laws of impact at high speeds are, etc. All that is clear, but can we stop at this point? If we do, we are confronted with this extremely interesting situation: the rational is controlled by the non-rational; the work of the reason, the expression of understanding, is controlled by things; the rational is controlled by the ontological.

It is not by accident that in the history of natural law (with the possible exception of Aristotle) the problem of the relation of nature to God is generally answered by the consideration that God is the author of human nature as well as of physical nature. In the eighteenth-century deism, for instance, there are rough formulas, metaphysically not very rich but retaining at least this much metaphysics: so long as God is there one does not have to be afraid that feathers will become heavy and lead light, that heavy bodies will go up and light bodies come down; the laws of nature are guaranteed by the divine stability. And by analogy from the physical nature, order and stability in the human universe, in the moral world, also are guaranteed by "Nature's God." There is at the root of all things, human as well as physical, an intellect and a will which offers an ultimate guarantee. Ultimately the order belongs to the rational. In this scheme we have the following three stages. First, natural law exists in our minds as a proposition. For instance, "Cheating in the execution of a contract is wrong by nature." But saying "by nature" we imply that natural law, before it is apprehended by the intellect, exists embodied in things; that is the second stage in the order of discovery. In the third stage, we are led to the recognition of an "author of nature" (this eighteenth-century expression, freed from its psychological, moral, political, and religious connections, is perfectly acceptable metaphysically) who is the legislator of nature. And thus the law which, *in the order of discovery*, exists first as a proposition in our minds, secondly as a way of being, thirdly and ultimately exists in the divine mind, where it takes on the name of divine law. There are a hundred reasons for opposition to natural law, but this is one of them and at certain times it may be the strongest: obligation in natural law does not hold unless the natural law exists in a state which is actually prior, but which is ultimate in the order of discovery —"this law is an aspect of God."

Among the proofs of God, the argument from the fact of obligation is of the same logical type as the proofs derived from the consideration of motion, or the consideration of causality, or the consideration of contingency, or the consideration of degrees of being, or the consideration of the order in nature.[15] As these other proofs, the proof from the fact of obligation is hard to manage and to expound in rigorous fashion. But this should not be held against the demonstration. There are innumerable examples from geometry and mathematics and logic illustrating the difficulty of proving their axioms and postulates. The difficulty does not necessarily mean that the proof is weak; it may merely mean, as in this case, that it is very difficult to master both the metaphysics of the subject and the logic of the proof in such a way as to make the argument "airtight." We do not propose to try it here; we shall merely outline the argumentation and suggest how and why it seems to be sound and conclusive and, accordingly, to admit of strict exposition.[16]

When we move from natural law existing as a proposition in our minds to natural law embodied in things, we have a subordination of the rational to the ontological. This seems unsatisfactory, but what is gained by placing a normative, regulating intellect behind the things and calling this the third stage? What about that regulating intellect itself? Does it also need to be regulated? If it does, then there is a fourth stage and a fifth stage and so on *ad infinitum*. We realize that in this kind of subordination driving a cause into infinity is to drive it into inexistence. There are cases where the notion of infinity has a very sound part to play. But we are not discussing Cantorian mathematics. And we are not discussing the question so timely in this space age: is there an infinite multitude of stars? Suppose we could travel in space with no limit of time. Would we be passing stars after stars for ever and ever? It is a fascinating question. Can there be an infinite multitude of stars? The most interesting answer is given in a few words by Thomas Aquinas. In one of his latest writings—in earlier works he had been inclined to think that an infinite multitude existing actually was an impossibility—his last word on the subject was that, after all, it had never been demonstrated that an actual infinite multitude was impossible.[17] This was said toward the end of the thirteenth century, and the impossibility has not been demonstrated since then. The notion of infinity is also present in the example of the generation of an egg by a hen, and the growth of a hen out of an egg. There is absolutely no reason why that series should not be infinite. True, some feel that there *must* be an end to it, but that is perhaps an effect of fatigue on the part of our imagination: an egg, a hen, an egg, a hen, an egg, etc., etc. There is, however, no rational necessity of an end in such a series, in this kind of subordination. And if we are looking for cause in it, we realize that by driving it into infinity we just drive it into inexistence.

It is objected that similar difficulties are met in the subordination of the rational to the ontological in theories of natural law, and that positing an intellect behind things, behind being, does not solve the problem of obligation because the series is infinite and the cause looked for is driven into inexistence. Faced with such a situation, it is not surprising that some would prefer to place natural law in the "nature of things," in the broader sense, and leave it at that.*

As remarked above, the proof of God from the fact of obligation is of the same logical type as the other aposterioristic proofs, i.e., from the facts of motion, efficient causality, contingency and necessity, degrees of being, and the order of the universe. The argument from the fact of obligation shares with these other philosophical proofs the formal principle of demonstration, viz., the necessity of a first cause which is pure act or being, itself subsistent in its own right.[18] Applied to our case, what ends the allegedly infinite series is an attribute, a characteristic of that pure act: the identity of "to be" and "to

---

* The problem remains unsolved. Imagine a painting being painted. There is a pack of hair, a ring of copper, a handle, and we call that a brush; behind the brush there is a painter. Now suppose the handle of the brush is a little longer. Do we still need a painter? Suppose the handle of the brush is indefinitely long. Well, we have driven the painter into inexistence, and we realize that nothing is being painted.

think." In our scheme of natural law existing—in the order of discovery—first in our minds, secondly in things, and thirdly as an aspect of God, the distance between the second and third stages is of minor relevance, even if not completely irrelevant.[19] What is decisive is whether or not we have to reach a stage where "to be" and "to think" are one; here the problem disappears and the obligation is explained. What is relevant is to understand what condition should be satisfied that the third stage will be better than any intermediary placed between it and the second stage, that it should be final; that condition is the identity of "to know" and "to be." Is that identity realized in God? I am sure it is. Aristotle, of whom we said in chapter 2 that he knew little about God, is quite certain on this point. He is undecided on the relation between God and the world because he has not worked out the metaphysical instruments needed to understand God as efficient cause and as knowing the world. And in order not to have to admit that God might be affected by (the counter-effect of) His creation and cognition—a pure Act being impressed upon makes no sense—Aristotle merely asserts that God moves the world in the capacity of final cause, as an object of desire moves desire (*Met.* 12.7. 1072a25). But concerning God Himself, Aristotle is explicit. For Aristotle, God is an act of intellectual consciousness, "thought, which is thought of thought." God's "to be" is an act of thinking whose object is itself (*Met.* 12.9.1075a).

Now that is perfectly in harmony with all we know about the relation of knowing and being. To express it in a few words, let us quote the famous page of Pascal on the thinking reed (*Pensées*, Routledge & Kegan Paul: London, 1950):

Man is but a reed, the weakest thing in nature; but a thinking reed. It does not need the universe to take up arms to crush him; a vapour, a drop of water is enough to kill him. But though the

universe should crush him, man would still be nobler than his de-
stroyer, because he knows that he is dying, knows that his universe
has got the better of him; the universe knows naught of that. (160)

All our dignity then consists in thought. We must look to that
in order to rise aloft; not to space or time which we can never fill.
Strive we then to think aright: that is the first principle of moral
life. It is not from space that I must get my dignity, but from the
control of my thought. The possession of whole worlds will give
me no more. By space the universe embraces me and swallows me
up like an atom, by thought I embrace the universe. (161)

It is a deservedly famous passage; the vocabulary, again, is
Cartesian, but that does not matter. What matters is that the
immensity of thought is expressed here with a rather unique
forcefulness. Do not be too bewildered by stories, whether fic-
tion or not, about space; an act of thought comprehends all
those things. With regard to my natural being I am restricted
in a hundred ways, especially in regard to duration, to power,
to versatility. But by thought there is something limitless, intrinsically infinite in me; by thought I can comprehend, I can
be, in some ways, all things (Aristotle *De Anima* 3.8.431b21).
And so we understand that in the Supreme Being, in the Being
where "what it is" and "to be" are one, there is identity of
"to be" and "to know." The infinity which is characteristic
of "to know" becomes ontological in the Supreme Being. If
there were such a thing as a definition of God, this would be
a good one. Of course, that is not a definition in any strict
logical sense, but as we have to use substitutes for a definition
of God this is perhaps the most profound of all: Being in
whom "to be" and "to know" are one and the same in all
possible respects. One can make a valid distinction between
the understanding of God and the will of God, between His
understanding and His love. It is not a real distinction, but it
is a valid distinction of reason, just as there is a valid distinc-

tion of reason between twice six eggs and one dozen eggs and the square root of 144 eggs. Those three are the same thing but we have diverse aspects grounding a valid distinction in our understanding. Mathematics would not exist if there were no valid distinction between twice six and twelve. Likewise, there is a valid distinction between the understanding and the love of God. But between the "to be" of God and the "to think" of God there is no distinction whatsoever; it is like two names designating exactly the same thing. And it is this identity of being and knowing that stops the regression to infinity in our search for the ground of obligation under natural law.

Some years ago there appeared in the distinguished journal *Philosophy of Science* an article entitled "Metaphysics of Design Without Purpose," considering for the n-th time the everlasting problem of finality in nature. *Philosophy of Science* is a publication whose inspiration may be described as independent Viennese; it is connected with what we shall soon be able to call "Old Vienna" logical positivism, but the connection is not dogmatic, it is a free one. The article made the following point:

> The problem of design is in no wise simplified by appealing to the idea of a designer outside of the system. Such an appeal simply moves the problem back one step, for either the designer designs by nature, to use an Aristotelian phrase, or designs because of some still further removed insistence for design. If the former alternative is taken, it is just as reasonable to say that the natural order is the condition of its own design. If the other alternative is taken, one is involved in an infinite regress, and the problem still awaits to engulf us; we have been granted only a temporary stay of execution.[20]

The author understood well that nothing is gained by merely placing an intellect behind things of nature; on the contrary, everything is lost because the foundation looked for, by being driven into infinity, is driven into inexistence. We have to stop at a thing which is directing by nature; so why not this thing, this organ, this planet, this universe? Since we have to stop somewhere, why should we not stop where we are and be satisfied with a design without a designing intellect? Answer: for the simple reason that in the things of nature—sulphuric acid, a plant of corn, Earth, universe, all behaving with remarkable regularity—there is no identity of "to be" and "to think" and no identity of "to be" and "to act." The privilege of the First Cause, the reason why there is no regression to infinity and why there is an intelligible stop—no matter how many phases we may have between the second and the third stages in our cognition of natural law—the privilege of the First Cause is the identity of "to be" and "to act" and "to think" which cannot be had anywhere else. The author of the article insisted that we must end with a thing which is designing by nature. Why place it outside the world and thus get lost in infinity? Why not place it, instead, in the world? Because, in order to place it in the world, we would have to support in that thing an identity of "to be" and "to act" and "to think," i.e., the predicates of God which, by clear evidence, are not realized in things of nature. These are mutable, multiple, stretched in space, subject to accidents, etc. Here we see how reasoning about finality in nature and reasoning about obligation ultimately converge. The ways are slightly different, but the logical structure and the end are the same. The facts of order in the universe and the facts of obligation under natural law, i.e., that our reason bows before things, both require rationally a transcendent First Being in whom "to be" and "to act" and "to think" are one and the same.

THE VARIATIONS OF NATURAL LAW

There remains the great question of the variations of natural law. It was first introduced at the very beginning, and it has been touched upon throughout this essay. As soon as we uttered the expression "natural law," we felt the power of certain objections—which do not originate in the twentieth-century anthropology, for they are as old as philosophic reflection on the subject. If there is a natural law of the human realm, if some actions are right and some actions wrong by nature, how do we account for so much diversity in mores, in institutions, in laws, and in judgments about the right and the wrong? That objection is contemporary with the birth of Greek philosophy; it certainly assumed a new power in the Renaissance, with the popularization of stories, more or less reliable, about strange aborigines; and in recent times it has acquired special force with social positivism and existentialism.

The question will be divided into five parts.[21]

1) So far as negative precepts are concerned, and in terms of what *is* right or wrong by nature—not in terms of what we actually know about the right and the wrong—the precepts concerning acts wrong by essence are possessed of unqualified universality. Let us explain. We leave out of the picture the question of our factual acquaintance with the right and the wrong; we are considering the things that *are* right or wrong by nature; we may or may not know that they are such. Next, we are considering *negative* precepts. Finally, the negative precepts under consideration concern acts wrong *by essence*. Here, and perhaps here only, we have unqualified universality.

The main and the most interesting difficulty concerns the definition of an act wrong by essence. Let us be aware that the externals being strictly identical, we may have two moral essences as different as the right is from the wrong. (Cf. *Sum.*

theol. i-ii.18. ad 3&4.) For example, under ordinary circumstances to take a thing without paying for it is stealing. Under circumstances of extreme necessity, it simply is not stealing. (*Sum. theol.* ii-ii.66.7;32.7. ad 2.) To take water from the water supply of my neighbor when he is not at home and in order to reduce my own water bill is stealing. If my house is afire and the neighbor's supply is the only source of water available to put the fire out, even if I should never be able to pay him for it, that water belongs to me under the circumstances. Extreme necessity *changes* the nature of the act. It is a very crude error to say that stealing is lawful in extreme necessity. Moral scepticism thrives on such confusion, which consists simply of a failure to notice that, the externals being identical, the moral essences of two acts may be as different as the right is from the wrong. At war, for instance, is there any difference between exposing oneself to certain death and taking one's own life? (*Sum. theol.* ii-ii.64.5. ad 3&5.) During the occupation of Europe by the Nazis this question certainly arose in an indeterminate number of concrete cases. Even the bravest are not likely to keep silent under prolonged, elaborate, scientific torture, and the secrets they cannot keep may result in the death of some companions and perhaps many other innocent persons. Is it not best, for the underground fighter caught by the Gestapo, to swallow a heavy dose of morphine or some cyanide? Many people thought not only that it was lawful, but that it was the thing to do, and they thought so not because they feared torture but out of a sense of responsibility for the secrets that they had to keep. To the objection that suicide can never be lawful, these people would point to military acts which are generally considered sheer heroism, like jumping out of a trench under machine-gun fire, or blowing up a bridge to stop the enemy tanks without having the time to pull away. Death here is as certain as it is by morphine or cyanide. Is there any difference between the two cases? A world of difference! Even though the externals may be identical, in one case there is the act of taking one's life, in the other the act of giving it. Between these two there is an infinite qualitative difference. What is wrong by nature can never be rendered right, but we shall have to be very cautious before we declare that a particular act is wrong by nature.

2) Let us, secondly, consider *positive* precepts, again relative to external acts. One principle covers all cases: any good act may become wrong by reason of the circumstances. The classical example is that proposed by Plato in *The Republic*: to return deposits is the right thing to do. But what if the deposit is a weapon and the depositor a criminal or an insane person? Or, what if the deposit is a large amount of money and the depositor a traitor? (*Sum. theol.* ii-ii.57.2. ad 1; i-ii.94.4.) In such cases there is an interference. Returning a deposit is an act good by essence but, whereas circumstances never can vindicate an act wrong by essence, an act good by essence always can be made wrong by the circumstances. (Cf. *Sum. theol.* i-ii.18.4. ad 3; *De Malo* 2.4. ad 2.) It seems as if the evil has a kind of diabolic privilege: the wrong cannot be made good, but the good can be made wrong. The example of Plato has to do with the circumstances known as *effect*. Returning this deposit, which is a weapon, to the regular owner who is a criminal or an insane person determines the effect that the weapon will be in the hands of an insane or criminal person. By reason of this circumstance, the intrinsic quality of the act is powerless; what is good in itself happens to be concretely wrong. In this world of contingency, all positive precepts relative to external acts are subject to interference. There can always be some defective circumstance which substitutes for a good action an action wrong by reason of the circumstances. Is the duty of respecting one's father a matter of natural law? Is it by nature or is it by human enactment that it

is good to respect one's father? No doubt, it is by nature. So far as the internal act of respecting one's father is concerned there is something universal which may be known more or less clearly, but that it is right by nature to respect one's father admits of no qualification. (*Sum. theol.* i-ii.100-5. ad 4.) What about external actions concerning one's father? Cases are conceivable in which it is permissible, good, necessary, obligatory to hit, perhaps to kill, one's father. Suppose, for instance, a violently criminal or insane man attacking his wife; the son rushes to her assistance and is perhaps forced to kill the assailant. That may be too bad, but it is not morally bad, and it does not mean that one can ever be disrespectful to one's father. There is an obvious duty to save innocent lives, and this duty may paradoxically interfere with the normal rule in which respect for one's father is embodied. The order of nature may always be affected and reversed by emergency. In this case there is a substitution: the person whom one is hitting is a murderer—who also *happens* to be one's father. In the words of Aristotle: a physician may also be a singer. Likewise, a father may also be a murderer. As physician, a man heals disease; as singer, he sings. The patient cannot say that he was cured by a singer. Likewise, a father can be a murderer, and a murderer can be a father. In the case under consideration, it is the murderer who is being prevented from taking an innocent life. Let the last example of the relation between positive precepts of natural law and the attending circumstances be the giving of alms. (*Sum. theol.* i-ii.20.1; *De Malo* 2.4. ad 2.) The definition of the act is: "To relieve destitution through free distribution." It is good by essence. But if it is done to show off, for vainglory, or in order to acquire disorderly power over helpless people, then it is wrong. Thus again, a thing substantially good becomes wrong on account of the circumstance *end*. The list of the circumstances, including the *effect* in

Plato's example, which may modify the essence of an act right by nature, is completed as follows: *who, when, where, by what means* (*Sum. theol.* i-ii.7.3).

3) Among the propositions which express what is right by nature, there is a valid distinction between premises and conclusions (*Sum. theol.* i-ii.94.4&6). Should it be said that the conclusions do not have the same necessity, the same immutability as the premises? This view is held by many, but that is strange logic. If the derivation of the conclusion is purely and simply logical, the conclusion derives unqualified necessity from the necessary premises. If we remain within the realm of moral essences, conclusions as well as premises are concerned with things that have intelligible, necessary constitution as moral determinations. If the premises are necessary and universal, the conclusions are the same. The following example is difficult, but it may be enlightening. Is it lawful to lend money for interest? The prevailing opinion and widespread institutional practice seem to answer this question in the affirmative. And yet, it would perhaps not be so easy to find an absolutely pure case of a loan for interest in the complex economic and financial processes of the modern society. Many a transaction may be shown by analysis to involve a contract not of loan but of association; also, extrinsic titles, such as damage, sacrifice, or service may be involved in what is for practical purposes considered a loan for interest. Assuming that there is neither association nor extrinsic titles, is it lawful to lend a man one thousand dollars, and after a year to collect, say, one thousand and sixty dollars? The proposition "Loaning money for interest is unlawful" is not self-evident. It has to be demonstrated through a middle term, which consists in showing that if one thousand dollars are lent and one thousand and sixty dollars collected—and there is absolutely no other qualification in the transaction—then the law of commutative justice has been violated. The law of commutative

justice is one of equality in exchange: an exchange is just when the values exchanged are equal (*Sum. theol.* ii-ii.61.2). It may be hopelessly difficult to ascertain their equality, e.g., to know how many pounds of wheat are equal to a pair of shoes. The social genius of mankind is continually devising new methods to improve the approximation to certainty with regard to the equality of exchanged values, but throughout these trials and errors we are guided by the certain knowledge that the only absolutely just exchange is the one in which the exchanged values are strictly equal. Now, using as a middle term this rule of commutative justice and considering what happens in the pure loan for interest, the conclusion is that to lend one thousand dollars and to get back one thousand and sixty dollars is to receive exactly sixty dollars in excess of what is due. In this deductive process the conclusion reached is as necessary as the law of commutative justice from which it is derived. Once again, even though it might be rather difficult to find a pure case of a loan for interest, this does not mean that the established practices are free from moral problems. We have reached a negative precept: do not practice loan for interest, it is contrary to the law of commutative justice. This conclusion, deductively connected with the law of commutative justice, is universal and admits of no exception (*Sum. theol.* ii-ii.78.1).

That a conclusion is always as necessary as the antecedent is almost a definition of a strictly logical connection. But the antecedents may be divided into those which do not and those which do involve a contingent condition. In a relation between antecedent and conclusion, the conclusion will always be as necessary as the antecedent. This division of which we speak does not concern the relation between antecedent and conclusion; it concerns the structure of the antecedent itself. When we consider such a problem as the lawfulness of loan for interest, we are dealing with moral essences in the state of abstraction which properly belongs to them. No contingent condition is involved; from premises concerning the requirements of commutative justice and from the definition of loan for interest, we infer the conclusion that loan for interest, precisely considered in its essence, in its distinctness, apart from qualifications and contingencies, involves a violation of the law of commutative justice. But we may have to deal with an antecedent implying a condition which is not always realized. See, for instance, the difference between suicide and adultery. The law which prohibits adultery does not concern bachelors. A bachelor may be an accomplice in adultery, but he cannot break a faith that he has never sworn to anybody. He can commit all sorts of crimes, but not that one; a subject, a matter, a condition is absent.

The case of what may be called "qualified antecedents" allows us to express more clearly the notion of a "law of nations." The expression is ambiguous; it has always been. It comes from Roman law where already it is confused. Recall the tripartite division discussed above: there are precepts of natural law that regard man as being; others regard man as animal; and still others regard man as rational agent. Sometimes by natural law Roman legists mean all three systems of precepts, but sometimes they include in "natural law" only the first two and use "law of nations" to designate those rules that pertain to man *qua* man, *qua* rational being. (Cf. St. Thomas, *In X Lib. Eth.* 1019.) But when "natural law" is used to designate all three divisions, what does "law of nations" designate? In modern times the term "law of nations" has come to designate international law, the law presiding over the relations among independent, sovereign states. Notice that to bring about some sort of order among sovereign nations not members of an organized community it is necessary to have recourse to positions commonly received in civilized societies: this is how the common law of civilized societies comes to be identified with international law. So long as there is no organized institutional community of nations, the only law which can hold is the one on which a number of independent communities happen to be in agreement. The case of natural law should be the same. In principle, the most diverse societies should be in agreement so far as the first premises of natural law are concerned. What about precepts that do not have the character of self-evidence but are derived from self-evident principles of natural law? We have just remarked that in such a deduction the antecedent may include a contingent condition. In fact, the contingent conditions that are commonly realized in developed societies constitute an entire and complex system. Vague as these terms may be, they help us perceive the normal source of international law. Its rules are deductions from natural law which indeed involve contingent conditions, but these contingent conditions are commonly realized when societies are sufficiently developed.

We use classical examples. One which seems to be very strong is the presence of an act of society distinguishing between what is marriage and what is not marriage and, accordingly, between legitimate and illegitimate children. Of course, there is certain contingency here. On a desert island we suppose that the natural law conditions for a valid marriage between a shipwrecked couple would be realized without the fulfillment of this precept of the law of nations, of "the common law of civilization." There is no civilization here; it takes more than one young man and one young woman to make up a civilization. In the absence of the general conditions of civilized society we find in this case an exception to an extremely general rule. The rule—that society, as it were, has a stake in marriage (*Sum. theol.* ii-ii.154.2; *Contra gentiles*, IV. 78.)—is indeed deduced from the axioms of natural law, but the antecedent in this deduction implies a presupposition that a commonly realized condition is in fact realized. It may not be. The most famous example of a precept of the "law of nations" so understood, is that of private property (*Sum. theol.* ii-ii.57.3; 66.2. ad 1; i-ii.94.5. ad 3). Is it by law of nature that things are owned privately, within certain limits, under the common circumstances of civilized life? It is. But notice that the statement is not particularly sharp: "within certain limits" and "under common circumstances of civilized life." In a very small tribe in a tropical forest, for instance, in the Amazon or Equatorial Africa, what meaning does private property assume? Are those common conditions realized which are needed in order that it be naturally right that there be some sort and some amount of private property? Perhaps not. Circumstances are conceivable in which doing without private property is the thing good and desirable and right, for the obvious reason that the common forms of civilization which make private property desirable are not realized. Wherever the normal conditions of civilized existence are realized it is right by nature, given those conditions, that there be some sort and some amount of private ownership. Do not try to obtain more precision, more specification, by way of logical connection. It will not work. For instance, an abominable inheritance tax is easily conceivable, but so is a perfectly just one. No doubt, the possibility of preservation of wealth in the same family from generation to generation is an important feature of social structure and development. Now modern inheritance taxes tend to destroy large estates and have certainly affected the status and meaning of wealth and private property. Can it be said that these reforms run counter to the principle of natural law requiring some sort and some amount of private ownership under normal conditions of civilization? Clearly the answer to this question is not to be found by way of deduction from the axioms of natural law. The issue is not one of logic but of prudential determination.

4) This is the fourth point: as soon as specific situations

and specific regulations are involved, there is absolutely no possibility of proceeding by way of logical connection. With regard to innumerable questions about the right and the wrong, the answer is obtained not by logical connection with principles but by determination of principles (*Sum. theol.* i-ii. 95.2; 99.4; *In X Lib. Eth.* 1023). Thus, the rule that honest families ought to be provided with the kind of independence without which family life is exceedingly restricted and precarious admits of indefinitely many embodiments, according to all sorts of contingencies, and a specific solution must be worked out in every particular case. In this process, after a few successful endeavors, some might be tempted to think that the problem has been solved, but it is soon found out that the circumstances have changed and that another determination must be improvised of the same inexhaustible axioms (*Sum. theol.* i-ii.97.1). That is one reason why scientific control of society will forever remain an illusion. The ideal of a science which would make it possible to realize the rational society conveniently ignores the obvious limitations of science, theory, logic, in relation to the life of contingency. The rational principle stipulating that when general conditions of civilization are realized it is desirable that there be some sort and some amount of private property does not specify either the kind or the amount, which change tremendously from place to place and from time to time. Would it be better if the steel industry were run by a federal agency? It might or might not be true—who is to say? The prudent! The connection here is not logical, it is prudential. And that is the end of all dreams of dictatorship by social scientists, by philosophers, by theologians, by any of those whose discourse is supposed to be a logical one. Logic goes this far: a particular worth attaches to some private ownership of earthly goods. But when we are asked to define, even in the roughest outline, the limits and kinds of private ownership, then we are in a flood of contingency and we have to find our way by methods that are appropriate to dealing with contingencies.

This point is of signal importance to this discussion. Even those things which in rough outline may be considered deductions from what is naturally right do not constitute standards or links by which the ultimate particular determinations might be logically connected with the first principles. For instance, marriage is an almost universal social institution, but there are many forms of marriage in the world and in history, and marriage without society is also possible. The particulars of regulation belong to prudental determination, not to logic. Logical connection is not completely severed: the prohibition of intercourse between very close relatives may be established by deduction. But what about third cousins? What about fourth cousins? Should marriage between them be prohibited? Should it be permitted with a special dispensation (so as to keep the case rare)? Should it be permitted without dispensation? (*Sum. theol.* ii-ii.154.8. ad 3; *Contra gentiles* III. 125.) Can a widow remarry a week after her husband dies, or should she wait ten months in order to be sure that a child who is really a son of the former husband will not be attributed to the new husband? Those things change quite normally from society to society; they do not follow from what is naturally right by logical connection. They are connected with the naturally right by way of prudential determination.

5) Lastly, we should keep in mind that the satisfaction of the inclinations of human nature may be more or less necessary, that the laws of human nature are necessary in a variety of degrees. A thing which is right by reason of what human nature is may be more certain than another thing. If, then, the one which is not so necessary appears less regularly in human societies, we should not be surprised. The great example here is polygamy *versus* monogamy. Is it right by nature that one man should have one wife? That is apparently the best form of mar-

riage. Is that absolutely indispensable? Considering the human inclinations that are satisfied by monogamy, it is clear that they do not possess the same kind of necessity as the inclinations to survive or to respect one's parents. Thus we have a basic division among things naturally right. The expressions "primary natural law" and "secondary natural law," commonly used by theologians, are acceptable. Primary natural law concerns what is naturally right in such a way as to be indispensable; secondary natural law concerns what is naturally right indeed but not indispensable (*Sum. theol.* i-ii.100.8; 97.4. ad 3). Elaborating on the example above: that there be only one wife is not as necessary as that there be only one husband (*Contra gentiles* III. 124). Where there is more than one husband fatherhood is uncertain and a great human good—knowing definitely who is the father of whom—is jeopardized. Polyandry, in fact, is a rather uncommon institution. Monogamy promotes great human goods by giving the woman the exclusive devotion of her husband. But the good of this exclusive devotion is not as necessary as certainty concerning fatherhood. The transition from polygamy to monogamy which may be observed in history, constitutes a normal progress from a state where only the more necessary laws of nature can be embodied in institutions to a state where institutions can afford to satisfy the less necessary and more lofty aspirations of nature. Divorce is a problem of the same type. One thing is sure: complete instability, no restrictions on instability, divorce at will, divorce granted as soon as one partner feels like terminating the marriage—is certainly contrary to natural law (*Contra gentiles* III. 123). Too great a human good would be destroyed by unrestricted instability in the relation of husband and wife. Between some restrictions, enough to give children a chance to be brought up in better than completely casual circumstances, and indissoluble marriage the difference is that between the more necessary and the less necessary.

(The factual meaning of the question is, of course, modified by the religious traditions of mankind, but this is a theological issue which does not pertain to this discussion.)

* * *

Concerning variations of natural law, two points pertaining to our knowledge of what is naturally right should be briefly stated in conclusion (*Sum. theol.* i-ii.94.4&6). First, such knowledge is progressive. There is absolutely no reason to postulate that man should have been created in a state of perfect acquaintance with what is naturally right; we do not postulate that he should be born with perfect acquaintance with the laws, say, of chemistry or biology. Thus there is nothing conclusive in the most common objection against natural law which notices that in a certain epoch a thing is considered to be naturally right about which the most intelligent and conscientious people were not so clear a few centuries before. That is normal; it reveals the law of progressivity, which is that of the human intellect. Secondly, we must be aware of the possibility of an abnormal blinding of our understanding of what is naturally right. We observe that in individuals all the time. There are people who upon inadvertently receiving a forged bill, for instance, have no fonder idea than to hand it on to another person. That is wrong by nature, contrary to the law of exchange. But probably not one shopkeeper in a thousand would bother about things like that. Now what happens to individuals can also happen to societies, so that if a practice considered highly immoral, wrong by nature, in one society is commonly received by mores and by laws and by institutions of another society, it does not follow that the case of what is naturally right is dubious. The possibility of corrupt judgment in a social group cannot simply be excluded. In fact, it is to be suspected that the judgment of every social group is blind or corrupt in some respect and to some extent.

The Future of Natural Law / 6

LET OUR DISCUSSION be concluded with a few remarks about future research in natural law. I wish again to call attention to the importance of the historical approach. The issue of natural law is one which is tangled by its historical adventures, and without keen awareness of those historical contexts it will never be untangled. There is a recent work on Rousseau and his forerunners by a French professor, Robert Derathé.[1] This book seems to have been immediately treated as a classic; it is likely to exert lasting influence. In the chapter about those forerunners of Rousseau who are known as the School of Natural Right (Grotius, Puffendorf, and a few others), Professor Derathé sets "natural right" as expressed by that school in opposition to "divine right." The School of Natural Right is thus said to be the expression of the secular society asserting itself against a theocratic concept of society, itself expressed in a theory of "divine right." It is melancholic to realize that concerning the notion of divine right the author is rather confused. Two or three different theories are completely mixed up, lumped together, identified. The expression "divine right," unless it is specified with care and lucidity, designates confusedly theories sharply at variance with each other. Bellarmine (1542-1621), for instance, uses the expression *ius divinum*, divine right, but his theory on the origin of civil power contrasts so sharply with that of James I (1566-1625), another famous theorist of divine right, that King James wrote a book to refute Bellarmine. It is difficult to see how the meaning and the historical significance of the School of Natural Right can be properly explained simply through an opposition to a School of Divine Right, which itself harbors contrasting doctrines. There is absolutely no chance of understanding such an issue as the influence of the School of Natural Right on the constitution of the secular society without going back to those historical antecedents and clarifying them first.

Another point to which I call attention is the inescapability of some theoretical presuppositions. It is vain and unprofitable to argue about the universality of natural right or natural law without a minimum of logic concerning the universals, concerning the meaning of universality, and there are other theoretical presuppositions which hold the key to some extreme difficulties. At the beginning of this essay we touched upon a number of doctrinal problems which are relevant to the theory of natural law. It may not have been the best possible method; sometimes it is better to go ahead with the issue under consideration and bring forth the presuppositions at the moment when they are most clearly indicated.

Thirdly, the need for *order* in the study of *the laws* should be strongly emphasized. I say "the laws," in the plural. Natural law is only one of them, and it is not the one with which we are primarily familiar. Let us begin by ascertaining our ideas concerning positive law, which is closest to our experience. This approach properly leads to the investigation of natural law. (And it involves the difficult theoretical problem of order in a set of analogates connected by proper proportionality.)

We spoke a great deal about judgment by way of cognition

and judgment by way of inclination. The distinction is of decisive importance in the theory of natural law, and quite indispensable in any theory concerning the more concrete ways of practical knowledge. The ultimate practical judgment is always determined by way of inclination. But we have seen that sound inclination, the good and honest will, is normally a way of apprehending also moral premises. Thus grasped, what is right by nature is expressed, "rationalized," in formulas of natural law. No need to insist on one of the most obvious conclusions of our research: there can be no scientific government. Speak of political science, if you please, provided it is understood that no proposition of scientific character will ever say the last word in government; it will always have the character of a high-placed premise. The ideal of scientific government, found in positivistic schools, has also been held by some believers in natural law. Skepticism toward natural law often is born of disappointment following such unreasonable expectations.

Concerning expectations about natural law, recall what was said about the function of philosophers in society and their choice between the pressures of ideology and the requirements of philosophy. Let us, however, insist on one point. From the very beginning of this exposition, we have tried to dismiss the ghost of certain objections, the main one of which is: if there were such a thing as natural law, it would be known to all men at all times, in all societies, in an equal degree of perfection. Though completely unwarranted, such postulations are given an appearance of validity by the formulas, sometimes a little too rough, not too carefully weighed, used by some theorists of natural law. Concerning cognition of natural law, we may assert what holds for human nature in general: human nature is progressive, which means both that it admits of progress and that it calls for progress. It does not mean that progress takes place inevitably. If there is progress, things are going on normally; if there is not, things are abnormal. Human nature achieves its own kind of perfection, never all at once, but always through what we very properly call a progression. Acquaintance with natural law is normally as progressive in mankind as anything else. Mankind did not know atomic physics or electronics by right of birth. There is no reason why the last word of natural law should be had all at once, any more than the last word of physics. The moral world is not less mysterious than the physical world. And if mankind advances rather slowly in the knowledge of the physical world, there is absolutely no reason to postulate that it should do better in the understanding of the moral universe, which is incomparably more mysterious because it includes the mystery of freedom. Why should accomplishment here be all at once rather than step by step, with possibilities even of regression? Einstein is reported to have said that if there is a hydrogen war, the next one will be fought with clubs. This may not be true, but it is not inconceivable that destruction be such that science and technology should also be destroyed. Thus one sees that even in science progress has two meanings and not three. It means that there is a possibility of progress, and it means that there is a demand for progress. It does not mean that there is a factual inevitability of progress.

Again, knowledge of natural law is not given all at once, either in the development of the individual man or in the development of mankind. In this respect the case of natural law is similar to that of crafts, sciences, music, poetry—all human cognitions and abilities. One does not become an excellent architect in one day, and mankind does not become excellent at building houses or temples in one generation. This should be absolutely clear: our knowledge of natural law is itself subject to a law of graduality in perfection, like everything else human. So understood, progress, here, also means that there is a demand for progress in the knowledge of natural law. When there is no progress in individual life, there is something wrong, something abnormal. The same holds for society and for mankind at large. There will never come a time when the demand for progress would stop. Nothing can be objected to the eighteenth-century idea of indefinite perfectibility of mankind, if it expresses a possibility and a demand. There is not the slightest reason to suspect that one day we shall have exhausted our potential with regard to the understanding of physical nature or with regard to the understanding of the moral world. What is questionable in the eighteenth-century theories of progress is the assertion of its inevitability. There is no factually necessary advancement in the knowledge of natural law or in any other human perfection. On the contrary, there is no reason why there should not be factual regressions, why there should not be aspects of natural law which were better understood three hundred years ago than they are among us today. If such is the case, there is abnormality, but it has never been demonstrated that such abnormalities are impossible. In fact, there is only one way to exclude the possibility of such abnormalities. It is to imagine that there exists within mankind a divine essence which realizes itself regardless of what happens in history. Such, indeed, was the postulation of the eighteenth-century and of many nineteenth-century theorists of progress. Whether called the human mind, the human spirit, mankind, humanity, nature, or evolution—in all cases it is a divine essence which is supposed to exist in mankind as a whole and to triumph, regardless of appearances, according to a law of necessary improvement. It is hardly necessary to elaborate on the mythological character of this theory.

Now a last word. We have just spoken of progressivity in our knowledge of natural law. There is also progressivity in the conditions which make it possible to apply the higher forms of natural law. For example, in recent years there have been efforts to suppress polygamy in several countries where such a reform would have been inconceivable a century ago. Today, it is embodied in civil law; they must have been thinking of it for more than one generation, and it probably was embodied already in common practice. It often happens that thinking or common practice are ahead of legal formulation of social reforms. A number of encouraging developments of a wider interest may be found in matters of justice in economic life. For instance, is collective bargaining a matter of natural law? Is it contrary to natural law that an employer should advertise, "Help Wanted," and then sign a contract with a worker couched in such terms that it can be terminated by either party without notice. Not so long ago this was common practice in industrial employment. The inequality of the parties was completely ignored. To us it seems quite clear that in case the employer terminates the contract he very probably will still have something to eat next week, whereas for the wage-earner, if his contract is involuntarily terminated, there is no guarantee that he and his family will not starve. Theodore Roosevelt, among others, understood early in this century not only that a wage-earner's labor was a "perishable commodity" but also that the labor problem was "a moral, a human problem" and that workers were organizing to secure "not only their economic but their simple human rights." [2] In the same period, however, there were people (and they still may be around) who could assert with great conviction that "the rights and interests of the laboring man will be protected and cared for, not by the labor agitators, but by the Christian men to whom God in His infinite wisdom, has given control of the property interests of the country." [3] So unions developed and the practice of collective bargaining was established. This is a very recent development and already not all the wrongs are on the same side in particular cases. The least that can be said is that realization of conditions under which justice in these economic relations can better be guaranteed is certainly in harmony with natural law. Again, despite the inequality between the employer and the wage-earner, there is not necessarily iniquity in their relation, because the employer may also be a fair and charitable fellow who would not use his right to terminate a contract except in extreme cases. Thus it cannot be said that in the old practice there was something purely and simply against natural law. But what ought to be said is that there is a dynamism of natural law demanding better guarantees of stability in employment when conditions are realized which both call for and make possible a better substantiation of what is naturally just.

Consider this last example: a man has reached the age of eighty years, cannot support himself, and has no family to take care of him. Is it a question of natural law whether helping this man should be organized by society rather than left to the fortuitousness of private initiative? The answer should not be in doubt, and it is the same for any of the hundreds of variations of the case. In fact, apart from war and peace, this is really the great problem of the present and the coming generations. What about old people, sick people, mentally sick people; what about victims of accidents at work and elsewhere; what about widows; what about crippled children; what about orphans? Is it right by nature that the help needed be institutional, or is it just as well to leave it to the charitable initiative of the people who happen to live next door, and who, upon hearing that there is a baby whose parents have just died, are going to take the baby and bring him up with their own children? I do not think that there is any doubt: that such help should be institutional is right by nature. This does not necessarily imply direct management by state authority; there is an indeterminate number of forms of organization admitting of diverse degrees of public control. What is important is that such help be not delivered to chance. It is also clear that such help cannot be organized all over the world and all at once. Historical reflection suggests that preceding the establishment of institutional forms, there is a gradual realization of conditions which make these institutions possible. Circumstances may be such that the help needed cannot be made institutional. We cannot imagine a "welfare state" in the sixth century, the century of great invasions. But that such help is necessary by reason of human nature and by reason of the contingency to which human nature is exposed—that cannot be doubted. Again, institutionalization and direct state control are not the same. I think that the meaning of what has been so vaguely talked about under the equivocal expression "social justice" in the last two generations is to be found in these propositions, and in the situation of the modern society. We have here, I believe, a very interesting perspective of progress in natural law. Not exactly by way of better understanding, but more precisely by reason of conditions which make it possible to accomplish, under more definite, more certain, more unmistakable rules, things that are naturally right and which in other ages were delivered to the fortuitousness of individual initiative, the whims of individual sentiment, and so on. My last words suggest that what is commonly called "social justice" admits of interpretation in terms of natural law. I believe that this is the task ahead of us. But it should be approached with extremely flexible and subtle instruments.

Notes

CHAPTER 1

1. (Leipzig: Hegner, 1936). An English translation is available under the title, *The Natural Law: A Study in Legal and Social History and Philosophy*, translated by Thomas R. Hanley (St. Louis: B. Herder Book Co., 1947).

2. *Ethics* 5. 7. 1134b18, translated by W. D. Ross: "Of political justice part is natural, part legal—natural, that which everywhere has the same force and does not exist by people's thinking this or that; legal, that which is originally indifferent, but when it has been laid down is not indifferent, e.g., that a prisoner's ransom shall be a mina, or that a goat and not two sheep shall be sacrificed, and again all the laws that are passed for particular cases, e.g., that sacrifice shall be made in honour of Brasidas, and the provision of decrees. Now some think that all justice is of this sort, because that which is by nature is unchangeable and has everywhere the same force (as fire burns here and in Persia), while they see change in the things recognized as just." *Rhetoric* 1. 13. 1373b4, translated by W. Rhys Roberts: "Particular law is that which each community lays down and applies to its own members: this is partly written and partly unwritten. Universal law is the law of nature."

3. *Discours sur l'origine et les fondements de l'inégalité parmi les hommes* (1755). *The Social Contract and Discourses*, translated by G. D. H. Cole (Everyman's edition), p. 208: "Every animal has ideas, since it has senses; it even combines those ideas in a certain degree; and it is only in degree that man differs, in this respect, from the

brute. Some philosophers have even maintained that there is a greater difference between one man and another than between some men and some beasts."

4. For a patient exposition of the Aristotelian and Thomist teaching on the universals, including a critique of Plato's and Duns Scotus' positions, see *The Material Logic of John of St. Thomas*, translated by Yves R. Simon, John J. Glanville, and G. Donald Hollenhorst (Chicago: The University of Chicago Press, 1955), chap. ii. The first thesis of Article 2, "Whether the Universal Understood Materially and As a Subject Is Found in the Real," opens as follows: "To the words and concepts expressive of universals there corresponds as object, truly and in an absolute sense, some entity or nature which is denominated universal. This nature does not exist in the real in the state of universality and abstraction, but, as a result of the abstraction performed by the intellect, it is so related to the nature existing in the object as not to include singularity. . . .

"In this abstraction there is no falsehood on the part of the intellect. Likewise, there is no falsehood in vision, which attains the color of the fruit without attaining its taste; it cannot be said that sight separates color from taste in the real world; all that can be said is that it does not put them together in knowledge. Thus, man is apprehended by the intellect without singularity, although in the real world man does not exist without it.

"In teaching this thesis we follow Aristotle (*Met.* 1. 6. 987a29), who continually fights the theory of Plato and also condemns by implication the opinion of the nominalists. See in particular St. Thomas, *Com.* on Met. 1. les. 10 [ed. Cathala, n. 158]. This is what he says about Plato's opinion: 'If the arguments of Plato are carefully examined, it is clear that what is erroneous in his thesis springs from the belief that the thing understood enjoys in its own existence conditions similar to those which pertain to our understanding of the same object' " (pp. 94-95).

On the modified Platonism of Duns Scotus see Article 3, "Whether Formal Unity, as Distinct from Singular Unity, Belongs to the Nature Prior to the Operation of the Intellect," pp. 102-114, especially p. 105 ff. "First thesis. No unity of a positive and absolute character, even though it be described as less than numerical unity, belongs to the nature considered in itself; it is impossible to say that such positive and absolute unity is bound up with numerical unity in the real. The nature considered in itself possesses only a negative formal unity, consisting in the negation of a division by formal principles."

5. *Ibid.*, pp. 96-97. "The nominalists contend that the universal concept signifying, for instance, 'man' or 'animal,' is a sort of collective noun which does not signify something that is one, but rather the

result of a grouping; the concept of man thus means all men, or all that to which the essence of man belongs. When I say: 'Man is an animal,' the meaning is: 'Everything which is man is animal,' or 'All men are animal.' For this reason, some seem to hold that what corresponds to the analogical concept of being is the whole collection of beings in a certain state of confusion.

"This way out is impossible for two reasons.

"1. When we use a universal noun as predicate, e.g., when we say: 'Peter is a man,' the sense would be that Peter is all men or that he is everything that is man, which is obviously false.

"2. When we use as a subject a common term without distributing it, as in the proposition 'Man runs,' the sense would be that all men run or that everything that is man runs. And so all indefinite propositions would be false. . . .

"Thus, a universal noun cannot in any way be a collective noun. It signifies something one, though abstracted from singularity."

6. *Time and Free Will*, translated by F. L. Pogson (London: George Allen and Co., Ltd., 1912), p. 140: "It is easy to see why the question of free will brings into conflict these two rival systems of nature, mechanism and dynamism. Dynamism starts from the idea of voluntary activity. . . . Mechanism follows the opposite course." *Matter and Memory*, translated by Nancy Margaret Paul and W. Scott Palmer (London: George Allen and Co., Ltd., 1912), pp. 13-14: "To ask whether the universe exists only in our thought, or outside of our thought, is to put the problem in terms that are insoluble, even if we suppose them to be intelligible; it is to condemn ourselves to a barren discussion, in which the terms *thought, being, universe,* will always be taken on either hand in entirely different senses. To settle the matter, we must first find a common ground on which combatants may meet; and since on both sides it is agreed that we can only grasp things in the form of images, we must state the problem in terms of images and images alone. Now no philosophical doctrine denies that the same images can enter at the same time into two distinct systems, one belonging to *science*, wherein each image, related only to itself, possesses an absolute value; and the other, the world of *consciousness*, wherein all the images depend on a central image, our body, the variations of which they follow. The question raised between realism and idealism then becomes quite clear: what are the relations which these two systems of images maintain with each other? And it is easy to see that subjective idealism consists in deriving the first system from the second, materialistic realism in deriving the second from the first." *Ibid.*, p. 240: "Dogmatism discovers and disengages the difficulties to which empiricism is blind; but it really seeks the solution along the very road that empiricism has marked out."

7. Aristotle. *Met.* 1. 2. 983a21; 938b1, translated by W. D. Ross: "We have stated, then, what is the nature of the science we are searching for, and what is the mark which our search and our whole investigation must reach. Evidently we have to acquire knowledge of the original causes. . . . We have studied these causes sufficiently in our work on nature, but yet let us call to our aid those who have attacked the investigation of being and philosophized about reality before us. For obviously they too speak of certain principles and causes; to go over their views, then, will be of profit to the present inquiry, for we shall either find another kind of cause, or be more convinced of the correctness of those which we now maintain." *De Anima* 1. 2. 403b20, translated by J. A. Smith: "For our study of soul it is necessary, while formulating the problems of which in our further advance we are to find the solutions, to call into council the views of those of our predecessors who have declared any opinion on this subject, in order that we may profit by whatever is sound in their suggestions and avoid their errors."

8. Cf. Leo Strauss, "On the Intention of Rousseau," *Social Research*, *XIV* (December, 1947), pp. 455-87. See also the essay by Bertrand de Jouvenel introducing Jean Jacques Rousseau, *Du contrat social* (Geneva: Constant Bourguin, 1947); Ernst Cassirer, *The Question of Jean Jacques Rousseau* (1932), translated by Peter Gay (New York: Columbia University Press, 1954); Robert Derathé, *Jean-Jacques Rousseau et la science politique de son temps* (Paris: Presses universitaires de France, 1950). Two other recent titles illustrate the point: John William Chapman, *Rousseau: Totalitarian or Liberal?* (New York: Columbia University Press, 1956) and Jean Starobinski, *Jean Jacques Rousseau: la transparence et l'obstacle* (Paris: Plon, 1957).

CHAPTER 2

1. "It would be well for those interested to reflect whether there now exists, or ever has existed, a wealthy and civilized community in which one portion did not live on the labor of another; and whether the form in which slavery exists in the South is not but one modification of this universal condition; and, finally, whether any other, under all the circumstances of the case, is more defensible, or stands on stronger ground of necessity. It is time to look these questions in the face. Let those who are interested remember that labor is the only source of wealth, and how small a portion of it, in all old and civilized countries, even the best governed, is left to those by whose labor wealth is created. Let them also reflect how little volition or agency the operatives in any country have in the question of its distribution—as little, with a few exceptions, as the African of the slaveholding States has in

the distribution of the proceeds of his labor. Nor is it the less oppressive, that, in the one case, it is effected by the stern and powerful will of the Government, and in the other by the more feeble and flexible will of a master. If one be an evil, so is the other. The only difference is the amount and mode of the exaction and distribution, and the agency by which they are effected." *Works of John C. Calhoun*, ed. Richard K. Crallé (New York: D. Appleton and Co., 1854-1857), vol. V, pp. 207-208. This quotation is the conclusion of Calhoun's "Report on the Circulation of Abolition Petitions." At about the same time, 1837, Calhoun was writing to James Hammond: "Our fate, as a people, is bound up in the question. If we yield we will be extirpated; but, if we successfully resist, we will be the greatest and most flourishing people of modern times"; quoted in Charles M. Wiltse, *John C. Calhoun: Nullifier, 1829-1839* (Indianapolis: Bobbs-Merrill Co., 1949), p. 366.

2. C. M. Wiltse holds that Calhoun's theory of slavery was derived, "perhaps subconsciously," from his "stern Calvinist heritage" (*John C. Calhoun: Nullifier, 1829-1839*, p. 365). Other biographers and historians blame Aristotle. For instance, Margaret Coit, *John C. Calhoun* (Boston: Houghton Mifflin Co., 1950), p. 288: "Without question Calhoun underestimated the mental potentialities of Negroes. ... Steeped as he was in the philosophy of Aristotle, he could not have felt otherwise. Had not Aristotle differentiated between the injustice of slavery based on 'conquest' and 'force of law' and the slavery of men who could obey reason, but were unable to exercise it?" (Aristotle *Politics* 1.5. 1254 b20, trans. B. Jowett: "For he who can be, and therefore is, another's, and he who participates in rational principle enough to apprehend, but not to have, such a principle, is a slave by nature.") But her own reference is to a eulogy by Robert Henry, Professor of Greek Literature in the South Carolina College, in *The Carolina Tribute to Calhoun*, ed. J. P. Thomas (Columbia, S. C., 1857), p. 234, where a footnote carries the Greek text. William S. Jenkins, *Pro-Slavery Thought in the Old South* (Chapel Hill: The University of North Carolina Press, 1935), p. 137: "The Aristotelian influence upon Southern thought was strong and may be traced through much of the pro-slavery literature. Probably to no other thinker in the history of the world did the slaveholder owe the great debt that he owed Aristotle." The footnote reads: "Specific examples of Aristotle's influence are too numerous to need citation, but see Calhoun's letter to A. D. Wallace, *Correspondence*, p. 469, where he acknowledges his debt to Aristotle." In this brief letter written on December 17, 1840, Calhoun advises a young man to learn to write and speak well, to study history and political economy, to acquire practical experience of public life, and to read a number of political works. Among these, Calhoun

recommends the *Federalist*, the Virginia and Kentucky Resolutions, Madison's Report to Virginia Legislature on the Alien and Sedition Act; he adds "... and the best elementary treatises on Government, including Aristotle's, which I regard as among the best." *Correspondence of John C. Calhoun*, ed. J. Franklin Jameson, Annual Report of the American Historical Association, 1899 (Washington: Government Printing Office, 1900), vol. II, p. 469. August O. Spain, *The Political Theory of John C. Calhoun* (New York: Bookman Associates, 1951), pp. 82, 263: "With Aristotle he believed...." "Aristotle was, of course, of great assistance in the defense of slavery." The reference again is to the above-mentioned letter to A. D. Wallace and this is apparently the only mention of Aristotle's name in Calhoun's published works.

George Fitzhugh was more explicit on Aristotle, but the way in which he acknowledged the debt seems to weaken the interpretations by Coit, Jenkins, and Spain (italics added): "*To our surprise, we found that our theory of the origin of society was identical with his, and that we had employed not only the same illustrations, but the very same words. We saw at once that the true vindication of slavery must be founded on his theory of man's social nature, as opposed to Locke's theory of the social contract.*" *Cannibals All! Or, Slaves Without Masters* (1857), p. 21; quoted in Francis Graham Wilson, *The American Political Mind* (New York: McGraw-Hill, 1949), p. 248n. Professor Wilson writes: "Southern thought returned to the Greek conception of an organic state, a society which was superior to individuals and which defined their liberty in the interest of the common good. Deep in the core of Southern thought, therefore, there was a denial of the rising principle of *laissez faire*, and of the idea of free competition. It can hardly be said that the South generally worked out this set of implications of its defense of slave society, but certain writers saw the problem in rather well-rounded contours. What Southern writers predicted was the failure of the new capitalism that was coming to dominate the North" (*ibid.*).

3. *Système de politique positive, ou traité de sociologie, instituant la religion de l'humanité* (4 vols.; Paris: L. Mathias, 1851-1854; *Catéchisme positiviste, ou sommaire exposition de la religion universelle, en onze entretiens systématiques entre une femme et un prêtre de l'humanité* (Paris, l'auteur, 1852); *Synthèse subjective, ou système universel des conceptions propres a l'état normal de l'humanite* (Paris, l'auteur, 1856). John Stuart Mill's evaluation of the "Later Speculations of M. Comte" (first published in *Westminster Review*, 1865) has been recently reprinted in a paperback: *Auguste Comte and Positivism* (Ann Arbor: University of Michigan Press, 1961). Mill, a contemporary, follower, and critic, wrote: "M. Comte's subjective syn-

thesis consists only in eliminating from the sciences everything that he deems useless, and presenting as far as possible every theoretical investigation as the solution to a practical problem. To this, however, he cannot consistently adhere; for in every science, the theoretic truths are much more closely connected with one another than with the human purposes which they eventually serve, and can only be made to cohere in the intellect by being, to a great degree, presented as if they were truths of pure reason, irrespective of any practical application" (p. 185). "One can only be thankful that amidst all which the past rulers of mankind have to answer for, they have never come up to the measure of the great regenerator of Humanity; mankind have not yet been under the rule of one who assumes that he knows all that there is to be known, and that when he has put himself at the head of humanity, the book of human knowledge may be closed" (pp. 180-81).

4. *The Doctor's Dilemma* (New York: Brentano's, 1920), "Preface on Doctors," pp. lxi-lxii: "Thus it was really the public and not the medical profession that took up vaccination with irresistible faith, sweeping the invention out of Jenner's hand and establishing it in a form which he himself repudiated. . . . If we had to decide whether vaccination was first forced on the public by the doctors or on the doctors by the public, we should have to decide against the public."

5. "Myths are not descriptions of things, but expressions of determination to act." George Sorel, *Reflections on Violence*, trans. T. E. Hulme (New York: Viking Press, 1914), p. 32.

6. Cf. Yves R. Simon, *The Road to Liberation* (*La Marche à la délivrance*), trans. V. M. Hamm (Milwaukee: The Tower Press, 1942), pp. 22-23: "I have avoided the use of the word 'myth' which has not succeeded so well with Sorel because of the ambiguities of which it could never be disabused. Repeated experiences have convinced me that one can do nothing to drive out of the mind of a reader the idea that a myth is a fable, an illusion, a mirage, and that to go to one's death under the impulsion of a myth is to give one's life for a cause which really is not worth the trouble. I have therefore substituted for the expression employed by Sorel that of 'heroic faith.' But this expression also presents certain disadvantages. While the word 'myth' suggests the idea of a belief which is false and in the last analysis mischievous, the expression 'heroic faith' suggests very strongly the idea of a belief that is true and that is destined to promote justice. Now, between the most vicious and the most virtuous forms of collective enthusiasm there are psychological and sociological analogies which render opportune the employment of a common term. That of 'mystique,' launched by Péguy on a celebrated page [Charles Péguy, *Notre jeunesse* (Paris: Gallimard, 1910), p. 26] would not be bad. We propose, then, to call heroic faiths those mystiques in which truth and justice pre-

dominate, and to reserve the name of 'myths' for those in which error and evil predominate."

7. For a more extensive analysis of "utopia" see *ibid.*, chap. ii.

8. Cognition is the subject of an early work of Professor Simon: *Introduction à l'ontologie du connaître* (Paris: Desclée de Brouwer, 1934). A posthumous volume is in preparation under the tentative title *Metaphysics of Knowledge*.

9. William James's definition of truth is well known: " 'The true' to put it briefly, is only the expedient in the way of our thinking, just as 'the right' is only the expedient in the way of our behaving. . . . We have to live today by what truth we can get today, and be ready tomorrow to call it falsehood." *Pragmatism* (New York: Longmans, Green, and Co., 1908), pp. 222, 223. James describes the pragmatic attitude as "one of looking away from first things, principles, 'categories,' supposed necessities; and of looking towards last things, fruits, consequences, facts" (pp. 54-55). But in the same work he also writes: "We are like fishes swimming in the sea of sense, bounded above by the superior element, but unable to breath it pure or penetrate it. We get oxygen from it, however, we touch it incessantly, now in this part, nov' in that, and every time we touch it, we turn back into the water with our course redetermined and re-energized. The abstract ideas of which the air consists are indispensable for life, but irrespirable in themselves, as it were, and only active in their redirecting function. All similes are halting, but this one rather takes my fancy. It shows how something, not sufficient for life itself, may nevertheless be an effective determinant of life elsewhere" (p. 128).

10. On the theory of prudence see Aristotle *Ethics* 6; Thomas Aquinas *Sum. theol.* i-ii. 57. 4,5,6; 65. 2; ii-ii. 47-56; John of St. Thomas *Cursus philosophicus* i-ii, disp. 16, a. 4,5 ([Paris: Vives, 1885], VI, 466 ff.); disp. 17, a. 2 (VI, 534 ff.).

11. This view corresponds to the motivation of Professor Simon's writings just before and during World War II. Deprived of the possibilities of combat and of political action, he deliberately reduced his theoretical philosophic research and gave himself to the task of reinforcing and purifying the ideology at birth in the Free World. *La Campagne d'Éthiopie et la pensée politique française* (2e ed.; Paris: Desclée de Brouwer, 1936); *La Grande crise de la République française, observation sur la vie politique des Français de 1918 à 1938* (Montreal: Editions de l'Arbre, 1941); in English, *The Road to Vichy*, trans. J. A. Corbett and G. J. McMorrow (New York: Sheed and Ward, 1942). *La Marche à la délivrance* (New York: Editions de la Maison française, 1942); in English, *The Road to Liberation*, trans. V. M. Hamm (Milwaukee: The Tower Press, 1942). *Par delà l'expérience du désespoir*

(Montreal: L. Parizeau, 1945); in English, *Community of the Free*, trans. W. R. Trask (New York: Henry Holt and Co., 1947). Strictly speaking, these books are neither speculative nor political; together with Professor Simon's numerous articles and lectures of that period, they could rather be offered as a demonstration of the philosopher's function in the city.

12. *Humanisme intégral* (Paris: Fernand Aubier, 1936), pp. 139-141; in English, *True Humanism*, trans. M. R. Adamson (New York: Charles Scribner's Sons, 1938), pp. 121-122.

13. E.g., Eduard Zeller, *Outlines of the History of Greek Philosophy*, 13th ed. revised by Wilhelm Nestle, trans. L. R. Palmer (London: Routledge & Kegan Paul Ltd., 1931), pp. 177-178: "The absolutely perfect being, the highest good, is also the end to which all things move and strive. On him the uniform order, the cohesion and life of the world depend. Aristotle did not assume the action of the divine will on the world or any creative activity or interference of the deity in the course of the world."

14. See below, pp. 142 ff.

15. See B. Gübbels, *Die Lehre des Aristoteles von den arbeitenden Klassen* (Bonn, 1927), p. 67. Cf. Yves R. Simon, *Trois leçons sur le travail* (2e ed.; Paris: Tequi, 1938), pp. 60-63.

16. *The Two Sources of Morality and Religion*, trans. R. Ashley Audra and Cloudesley Brereton (New York: Henry Holt and Company, 1935). The reference certainly does not imply endorsement of Bergson's thesis; it is rather a case of recognizing a concept which may serve as a starting point for philosophic dialogue. Bergson solves the contrast between the closed and the open society, harboring the closed and the open souls, formed respectively by "social pressure" and "impetus of love," as follows: "Reinstate the duality of origin, and the difficulties vanish. Nay, the duality itself merges into a unity, for 'social pressure' and 'impetus of love' are but two complementary manifestations of life, normally intent on preserving generally the social form which was characteristic of the human species from the beginning, but, exceptionally, capable of transfiguring it, thanks to the individuals who each represent, as the appearance of a new species would have represented, an effort of creative evolution" (p. 87). Bergson is mystical, stresses emotions as a historic force, and believes these emotions to be an expression of a cosmic élan. While also recognizing the importance of great men, Professor Simon's approach may, by contrast, be described as factual, allowing reason a role in history, and considering history itself primarily a human affair.

17. *Das Naturrecht in Thomistischer Beleuchtung* (Freiburg in der Schweiz: Verlag der Paulusdruckerei, 1944), p. 43.

18. *De jure belli ac pacis*, Prolegomena, para. 11.
19. See Yves R. Simon, *Philosophy of Democratic Government* (Chicago: The University of Chicago Press, 1951), pp. 155-176. The work is also available in paperback edition, Phoenix Books, The University of Chicago Press, 1961, same pagination.
20. See Yves R. Simon, *Community of the Free*, ch. ii.
21. See Yves R. Simon, *A General Theory of Authority* (Notre Dame: University of Notre Dame Press, 1962), pp. 60-79.

CHAPTER 3

1. See below, pp. 118-125.
2. See Emile Meyerson, *Identity and Reality*, trans. Kate Loewenberg (London: George Allen & Unwin, 1930), chap. ii, "Mechanism." In the "Conclusions," Meyerson writes: "It is permissible, therefore, to state that science really tends toward the reduction of all phenomena to a universal mechanism or atomism, defining these terms so as to include electrical theories, and remembering that the causality of being, so near a relative of the causality of becoming, demands that the elementary particles be made of a single matter possessing only a minimum of qualities, in such a way that it may be, to a certain extent, identified with space or its hypostasis, ether. Not that this reduction is really possible, nor that we can believe that this atomism constitutes the essence of things, nor that it is capable of offering a system free from contradiction—but because it is, amongst all the images which our intellect is capable of conceiving, the only one, which, satisfying at least to a certain degree our tendency in the direction of identity, offers at the same time real and sometimes surprising agreements with phenomena. It is, therefore, in following up this image, in rendering it more and more adequate to the facts, that we have the greatest chance of knowing these latter better. In other words, reduction of mechanism and atomism is not in itself an end but a means" (pp. 410-11). On Meyerson, see Jacques Maritain, *Philosophy of Nature* (New York: Philosophical Library, 1951), pp. 62-70.
3. *Meditations*, VI; *Principles*, Second Part. See also Smith, *New Studies in the Philosophy of Descartes: Descartes as Pioneer* (London, Macmillan, 1952) and compare Jacques Maritain, *The Dream of Descartes*, trans. Mabelle L. Andison (New York: Philosophical Library, 1944).
4. *Principles*, Second Part, xxiii: "There is therefore but one matter in the whole universe, and we know this by the simple fact of its being extended. All the properties which we clearly perceive in it may be reduced to the one, viz., that it can be divided, or moved according to its parts, and consequently is capable of all these affections which we

perceive can arise from the motion of its parts. For its partition by thought alone makes no difference to it; but all the variation in matter, or diversity in its forms, depends on motion. This the philosophers have doubtless observed, inasmuch as they have said that nature was the principle of motion and rest, and by nature they understood that by which all corporeal things become such as they are experienced to be." *Philosophical Works of Descartes*, trans. E. S. Haldane and G. R. T. Ross (Dover Publications, 1955), vol. I, p. 265.

5. *Principles*, Second Part, lxiv; ibid., p. 269.

6. *Discourse on Method*, V; *ibid.*, pp. 115-8. Letters to the Duke of Newcastle, November 1646, and to Henry Moore, February 1649 (A.T. iv, pp. 573-6; v, pp. 276-9).

7. Cf. Smith, *New Studies*, pp. 159-60: "For Descartes ... the mental and the physical differ *toto genere*; each is the opposite of the other. No other natural entity serves to parallel or illustrate even distantly the union of mind and body; it is altogether unique. Man is the only point, in the whole realm of nature, at which we find them conjoined; and though thus conjoined, they are never *substantially* one; it is a union only *quodam modo*, i.e., only quasi-substantial. Also, even as thus conceived, the degree and manner of the union is utterly beyond our powers of comprehension. Sense-experience suffices to convince us of its reality; but neither sense nor pure understanding affords us any data enabling us genuinely to comprehend even so much as its bare possibility." Maritain, *The Dream of Descartes*, p. 179: "Cartesian dualism breaks man up into two complete substances, joined to one another no one knows how: on the one hand, the body which is only geometric extension; on the other, the soul which is only thought —an angel inhabiting a machine and directing it by means of the pineal gland."

8. *Ethics*, Part II, "Concerning the Nature and Origin of the Mind," Proposition 7, trans. A. Boyle (Everyman's edition), pp. 41-42: "The order and connection of ideas is the same as the order and connection of things. *Proof.*—This is clear from Ax. 4, Part I. For the idea of everything that is caused depends on the knowledge of the cause of which it is an effect. *Corollary.*—Hence it follows that God's power of thinking is equal to his actual power of acting; that is, whatever follows formally from the infinite nature of God, follows also invariably objectively from the idea of God in the same order and connection. *Note.*—Before we proceed any further, let us call to mind what we have already shown above: that whatever can be perceived by infinite intellect as constituting the essence of substance, invariably appertains to one substance alone; and consequently thinking substance and extended substance are one and the same thing, which is now comprehended through this and now through that attribute."

9. "Third Explanation" of the "New System of the Nature of Substances and of the Communication between them, as well as of the Union there is between Soul and Body." *The Monadology and other Philosophical Writings*, trans. Robert Latta (London: Oxford University Press, 1898), pp. 331-334.

10. *Neuf leçons sur les notions premières de la philosophie morale* (Paris: Desclée de Brouwer, 1951). See in particular pp. 33, 38-66. The gist of this theory is forcefully expressed in the following sentences (p. 47): "Thus, moral values are a particular area, an area peculiar to human conduct, in the general domain of values antecedently acknowledged by the theoretical reason. If we consider things from this angle, we realize that the case of ethical values is not exceptional and that it belongs to an already known system, normal in all respects. Theoretical knowledge, metaphysics, philosophy of nature, the sciences of nature, medicine, logic overflow with value-judgments concerning the greater or lesser degree of a quality that should be there."

11. See *Kant's Critique of Practical Reason and Other Works on the Theory of Ethics*, trans. T. A. Abbott (6th ed.; London: Longmans, Green and Co., 1906).

12. Louis Gabriel Ambroise, vicomte de Bonald, *Oeuvres* (Brussels, 1845), vol. II, p. 86: "The savage state is the native state; hence it is weak and imperfect; either it is destroyed or it becomes civilized. The civilized state is the developed, fulfilled, perfect state; it is the natural state." An Iroquois is "*un homme natif*"; Bossuet, Fenelon, and Leibnitz are "*des hommes naturels*" (p. 87). Rousseau is the "novelist of the savage state, the detractor of the civilized state" (*ibid.*); quoted in Mary Hall Quinlan, *The Historical Thought of the Vicomte de Bonald* Washington, D.C.: The Catholic University of America Press, 1953), pp. 15-16.

13. "In virtue of which we hold that there can be no fact real or existing, no statement true, unless there be a sufficient reason, why it should be so and not otherwise, although these reasons usually cannot be known to us." *Monadology*, 32; Latta, p. 235.

14. E.g., Marcus Aurelius *Meditations* iv. 40, 45 (trans. G. Long): "Constantly regard the universe as one living being, having one substance and one soul; and observe how all things have reference to one perception, the perception of this one living being; and how all things act with one movement; and how all things are the co-operating causes of all things which exist; observe too the continuous spinning of the thread and the contexture of the web." "In the series of things those which follow are always aptly fitted to those which have gone before; for this series is not like a mere enumeration of disjointed things, which has only a necessary sequence, but it is a rational connection: and as all existing things are arranged together harmoniously, so the things

which come into existence exhibit no mere succession, but a certain wonderful relationship." The Stoic practical teaching is summed up in v. 8: "For two reasons then it is right to be content with that which happens to thee; the one, because it was done for thee and prescribed for thee, and in a manner had reference to thee, originally from the most ancient causes spun with thy destiny; and the other, because even that which comes severally to every man is to the power which administers the universe a cause of felicity and perfection, nay even of its very continuance. For the integrity of the whole is mutilated, if thou cuttest off anything whatever from the conjunction and the continuity either of the parts or of the causes. And thou dost cut off, as far as it is in thy power, when thou art dissatisfied, and in a manner triest to put anything out of the way." Whitney J. Oates (ed.), *The Stoic and Epicurean Philosophers* (New York: Random House, 1940), pp. 514, 521.

15. Part III, "Concerning the Origin and Nature of the Emotions," Introduction (Everyman's edition), p. 84: "Nothing happens in nature which can be attributed to a defect of it: for nature is always the same and one everywhere, and its ability and power of acting, that is, the laws and rules of nature according to which all things are made and changed from one form into another, are everywhere and always the same, and therefore one and the same manner must there be of understanding the nature of all things, that is, by means of universal laws and rules of nature. . . . And so I shall treat of the nature and force of the emotions, and the power of the mind over them, in the same manner as I treated of God and the mind in the previous parts, and I shall regard human actions and desires exactly as if I were dealing with lines, planes, and bodies."

16. Part IV, Proposition 67: "A free man thinks of nothing less than of death, and his wisdom is a meditation not of death but of life"; *ibid.*, p. 187.

17. Part II, Proposition 49: "There is in the mind no volition or affirmation and negation save that which the idea, in so far as it is an idea, involves." The lengthy note (after the usual proof and corollary) concludes: "It remains that I should point out how much this doctrine confers advantage on us for the regulating of life. . . . In so far as it teaches us in what manner we should act with regard to the affairs of fortune or those which are not in our power, that is, with regard to those things which do not follow from our nature: namely, that we should expect and bear both faces of fortune with an equal mind; for all things follow by the eternal decree of God in the same necessity as it follows from the essence of a triangle that its three angles are equal to two right angles . . ." (Everyman's edition, p. 80-81). In Part IV, "On Human Servitude, or the Strength of the Emotions,"

Proposition 69 asserts that "the virtue of a free man appears equally great in refusing to face difficulties as in overcoming them" (p. 188). The note to Proposition 73 ("A man who is guided by reason is more free in a state where he lives according to common law than in solitude where he is subject to no law.") reads in part: "A strong man considers this above all things, that everything follows from the necessity of divine nature; and accordingly, whatever he thinks to be a nuisance or evil, and whatever, moreover, seems to him impius, horrible, unjust, or disgraceful, arises from the fact that he conceives these things in a disturbed, mutilated, and confused manner: and on this account he endeavours to conceive things as they are in themselves, and to remove obstacles from true knowledge, as, for example, hatred, rage, envy, derision, pride, and the other emotions of this kind which we have noted in the previous propositions: and therefore he endeavours as much as he can, as we said, to act well and rejoyce. How far human virtue lends itself to the attainment of this, and what it is capable of, I shall show in the next part" (p. 191). *Ethics* concludes with a note to the proposition that virtue is its own reward (Part V, Proposition 42): "Thus I have completed all I wished to show concerning the power of the mind over emotions or the freedom of the mind. From which it is clear how much a wise man is in front and how stronger he is than an ignorant one, who is guided by lust alone.... The wise man, in so far as he is considered as such, is scarcely moved in spirit: he is conscious of himself, of God, and things by a certain eternal necessity, he never ceases to be, and always enjoys satisfaction of mind. If the road I have shown to lead to this is very difficult, it can yet be discovered. And clearly it must be very hard when it is so seldom found. For how could it be that it is neglected practically by all, if salvation were close at hand and could be found without difficulty? But all excellent things are as difficult as they are rare" (p. 224).

18. *La Physique quantique restera-t-elle indéterministe?* (Paris: Gauthier-Villars, 1953).

19. See Yves R. Simon, *Prévoir et savoir, études sur l'idée de la necessité dans la pensée scientifique et en philosophie* (Montreal: Editions de l'Arbre, 1944).

20. Letter to Menoeceus, Diogenes Laertius X 133; *The Stoic and Epicurean Philosophers*, p. 33.

21. Lucretius *De Rerum Natura* II 216-225, trans. H. A. J. Munro: "This point too herein we wish you to apprehend: when bodies are borne downwards sheer through void by their own weights, at quite uncertain times and uncertain spots they push themselves a little from their course: you just and only just can call it a change of inclination. If they were not used to swerve, they would all fall down, like drops of rain, through the deep void, and no clashing would have been begotten

nor blow produced among the first-beginnings: thus nature never would have produced aught." Further, lines 277-293: "Do you see then in this case that, though an outward force often pushes men on and compels them frequently to advance against their will and to be hurried headlong on, there yet is something in our breast sufficient to struggle against and resist it? And when too this something chooses, the store of matter is compelled sometimes to change its course through the limbs and frame, and after it has been forced forward, is reined in and settles back into its place. Wherefore in seeds too you must admit the same, admit that besides blows and weights there is another cause of motions, from which this power of free action has been begotten in us, since we see that nothing can come from nothing. For weight forbids that all things be done by blows through as it were an outward force; but that the mind itself does not feel an internal necessity in all its actions and is not as it were overmastered and compelled to bear and put up with this, is caused by a minute swerving of first-beginnings at no fixed part of space and no fixed time." Oates, *The Stoic and Epicurean Philosophers*, p. 95, 96.

22. See Yves R. Simon, *Traité du libre arbitre* (Liège: Sciences et lettres, 1951); also, "On the Foreseeability of Free Acts," *The New Scholasticism*, vol. XXII, No. 4 (October, 1948), pp. 357-370.

23. See below, ch. v.

CHAPTER 4

1. See below, pp. 110-111.

2. See *The Material Logic of John of St. Thomas*, Question 25, "On Demonstration," especially Article 1, "On Aristotle's Definition of Demonstration," pp. 472-481.

3. See, for example, Robert Derathé, *Le Rationalisme de J.-J. Rousseau* (Paris: Presses universitaires de France, 1948).

4. See Jacques Maritain, *Distinguer pour unir ou les degrés du savoir* (4th ed.; Paris: Desclée de Brouwer, 1946), pp. 120-128; also, *Philosophy of Nature*, pp. 102-114.

5. "Discourse on the Method of Rightly Conducting the Reason and Seeking for Truth in the Sciences," Part II, in *The Philosophical Works of Descartes*, trans. Haldane and Ross (Dover Publications) vol. I. Descartes explains the rules at which he had arrived: "The first of these was to accept nothing as true which I did not clearly recognize to be so; that is to say, carefully to avoid precipitation and prejudice in judgments, and to accept in them nothing more than what was presented to my mind so clearly and distinctly that I could have no occasion to doubt it. The second was to divide up each of the difficulties which I examined into as many parts as possible, and as seemed

requisite in order that it might be resolved in the best manner possible. The third was to carry on my reflections in due order, commencing with objects that were the most simple and easy to understand, in order to rise little by little, or by degrees, to knowledge of the most complex, assuming an order, even if a fictitious one, among those which do not follow a natural sequence relatively to one another. The last was in all cases to make enumerations so complete and reviews so general that I should be certain of having omitted nothing" (p. 92). In "The Principles of Philosophy," Part I, Principle xlv, Descartes explains further: "I term that clear which is present and apparent to an attentive mind, in the same way as we assert that we see objects clearly when, being present to the regarding eye, they operate upon it with sufficient strength. But the distinct is that which is so precise and different from all other objects that it contains within itself nothing but what is clear" (*ibid.*, p. 237).

6. See *The Material Logic*, Question 1, "On the Nature and Domain of Logic"; Question 2, "On the Logical Being of Reason"; and Question 24, "On Cognitions Anterior to Demonstration and on Premises" (pp. 1-59; 59-89; 436-471).

7. *Sum. theol.* i-ii. 6. 2, trans. A. C. Pegis. The title of the article is "Whether there is anything voluntary in irrational animals?" The answer reads in part: "Now knowledge of the end is twofold, perfect and imperfect. Perfect knowledge of the end consists in not only apprehending the thing which is the end, but also knowing it under the aspect of end, and the relationship of the means to that end. And such a knowledge of the end belongs to none but the rational nature.— But imperfect knowledge of the end consists in a mere apprehension of the end, without knowing it under the aspect of end, or the relationship of an act to the end. Such knowledge of the end is exercised by irrational animals, through their senses and their natural estimative power."

8. *De Anima* 3.10. 433a13; 11. 434a16. Cajetan *In Sum. theol.*, i-ii. 90. 1 ad 2.

9. *Amor transit in conditionem objecti*, John of St. Thomas *Curs. theol.* i-ii, d. 18, a. 4, ed. Vives, VI, 683; quoted in Yves R. Simon, "An Introduction to the Study of Practical Wisdom, " *The New Scholasticism*, vol. XXXV, no. 1 (January, 1960), p. 21. The subject was first treated by Professor Simon in an early work, *Critique de la connaissance morale* (Paris: Desclée de Brouwer, 1934). A posthumous volume is in preparation under the tentative title *Critique of Practical Knowledge*.

10. See Simon, *Philosophy of Democratic Government*, pp. 19-35, *A General Theory of Authority* (Notre Dame: University of Notre Dame Press, 1962), pp. 31-50.

11. See Yves R. Simon, "From the Science of Nature to the Science of Society," *The New Scholasticism*, vol. XXVII, no. 3 (July, 1953), pp. 280-304.

12. See *A General Theory of Authority*, pp. 23-29.

13. See Yves R. Simon, "On Art and Morality," *The New Scholasticism*, vol. XXXV, no. 3 (July, 1961), pp. 338-341.

14. *Sum. theol.* i-ii. 57.4, "Whether Prudence Is a Distinct Virtue from Art?" trans. A. C. Pegis: "Where the nature of virtue differs, there is a different kind of virtue. Now it has been stated above that some habits have the nature of virtue, through merely conferring ability for a good work; while some habits are virtues, not only through conferring ability for a good work, but also through conferring the use. But art confers the mere ability for good work, since it does not regard the appetite, whereas prudence confers not only ability for a good work, but also the use, for it regards the appetite, since it presupposes the rectitude of the appetite. The reason for this difference is that art is the *right reason of things to be made*, whereas prudence is the *right reason of things to be done*. Now *making* and *doing* differ, as is stated in *Metaph.* ix [8. 1050a 30], in that *making* is an action passing into external matter, *e.g. to build, to saw* and so forth; whereas *doing* is an action abiding in the agent, *e.g. to see, to will*, and the like. Accordingly, prudence stands in the same relation to such human actions, consisting in the use of powers and habits, as art does to external makings; since each is the perfect reason about the things with which it is concerned. But perfection and rectitude of reason in speculative matters depend on the principles from which reason argues; just as we have said above that science depends on and presupposes understanding, which is the habit of principles. *Now in human acts ends are what principles are in speculative matters*, as is stated in *Ethics* vii [8. 1151a 16]. Consequently, it is requisite for prudence, which is right reason about things to be done, that man be well disposed with regard to ends; and this depends on the rectitude of his appetite. Therefore, for prudence there is need of moral virtue, which rectifies the appetite. On the other hand, the good of things made by art is not the good of man's appetite, but the good of the artificial things themselves, and hence art does not presuppose rectitude of the appetite. The consequence is that more praise is given to a craftsman who is at fault willingly, than to one who is unwillingly; whereas it is more contrary to prudence to sin willingly than unwillingly, since rectitude of the will is essential to prudence, but not to art.—Accordingly, it is evident that prudence is a virtue distinct from art."

15. The distinction between transitive and immanent actions is explained by Aristotle in *Met.* 9. 8. 1050a 30, trans. W. D. Ross: "Where, then, the result is something apart from the exercise, the

actuality is in the thing that is being made, e.g. the act of building is in the thing that is being built and that of weaving in the thing that is being woven, and similarly in all other cases, and in general the movement is in the thing that is being moved; but where there is no product apart from the actuality, the actuality is present in the agents, e.g. the act of seeing is in the seeing subject and that of theorizing in the theorizing subject and the life is in the soul (and therefore well-being also; for it is a certain kind of life)."

16. *Works of William E. Channing* (Boston: American Unitarian Association, 1903), p. 700; the context is a discussion of "Slavery."

17. *Ibid.*, p. 701.

18. *Liberty in the Modern State* (New York: The Viking Press, 1949), p. 39.

19. See *Philosophy of Democratic Government*, ch. 3, "Sovereignty in Democracy."

CHAPTER 5

1. See above, footnote on pp. 69-70.

2. See Yves R. Simon, "On Order in Analogical Sets," *The New Scholasticism*, vol. XXXIV, no. 1 (January, 1960), pp. 1-42.

3. For a concise statement to the contrary, ignoring the pragmatists' position, see Yves R. Simon, "Thomism and Democracy," in *Science, Philosophy, and Religion: Second Symposium* (New York: Conference on Science, Philosophy and Religion in Their Relations to the Democratic Way of Life, 1942), pp. 258-272.

4. See *Sum. theol.* i-ii. 97, "On Change in Laws."

5. See, for example, the citations from the most varied sources in Iredell Jenkins, "The Matrix of Positive Law," *Natural Law Forum*, vol. VI (1961), pp. 1-50, especially pp. 3-16.

6. Cf. A. P. d'Entreves, *Natural Law: An Introduction to Legal Philosophy* (London: Hutchinson's University Library, 1951), chap. 3, "A Theory of Natural Rights." See also Peter J. Stanlis, *Edmund Burke and the Natural Law* (Ann Arbor: University of Michigan Press, 1958).

7. *Ethics*, Part III, Proposition 6.

8. Trans. and ed. H. M. Parshley (New York: Alfred A. Knopf, 1953).

9. Abraham Stone, "A New History of Women, with Special Reference to Their Oppression by Men," vol. CLXXXVIII, no. 4 (April, 1953), pp. 105-107.

10. For example: "Nature was conceived by Kant as the existence of things in so far as that existence is determined according to universal laws. Man, Kant holds, as a creature of nature is subject to these laws

in so far as he *is* a creature of nature and nothing more. But on the basis of the fact of civilization and more particularly man's moral experience, also taken as a fact, Kant claims that man is something more than a being of nature; he is a being of freedom or a being in whose life reason can have a determining influence. In the *Anthropology*, Kant lays great stress upon a distinction between two approaches to the study of man, a *physiological* and a *pragmatic* approach. The first type has to do, he says, 'with what nature makes of man,' while the second concerns what man, 'as a free agent, makes—or rather can and ought to make—of himself.' And, as is well known, it is what man *ought* to make of himself which is decisive for Kant's view. As Cassirer expresses it, 'Kant never takes the idea of the *homme naturel* in a purely scientific or historical sense, but rather ethically and teleologically. . . . Kant looks for constancy not in what man is but in what he *should be*.' " [Ernest Cassirer, *Rousseau, Kant, Goethe* (Princeton, 1945), p. 20.] John S. Smith, "The Question of Man," in Charles W. Hendel *et al., The Philosophy of Kant and Our Modern World* (New York: The Liberal Arts Press, 1957), p. 20.

11. The editor feels that it is appropriate to quote here from a remembrance by Leo R. Ward: "Yves Simon, who died in South Bend on Ascension Thursday, was one of the distinguished philosophers of the twentieth century. He was also an extraordinary teacher. . . . Many students will say they never had a teacher to match him. He was sick for two years, but his devotion to teaching and study went right on. . . . His last lecture was his most famous and most memorable. He was at that time a very sick man, but he had promised the lecture, and he lavished himself both on the preparation and the giving of it. It was touching and unforgettable. He could not walk or stand, and had to be carried onto the platform and propped up in pillows. He was suffering terribly. But the lecture did not suffer, and his hearers did not suffer. For two hours he lectured and answered questions with charm and with tremendous vigor, and every member of the audience, most of whom had never seen him before, waited and listened to every word. . . . Yves Simon did not keep his scientific philosophic work in one compartment and his life of faith sealed off in another. He accepted freely and effectively what it means—in theory and in practice—to be a Christian philosopher." "Yves Simon, Philosopher," *Commonweal*, vol. LXXIV, no. 14 (June 30, 1961), pp. 351-352.

12. Aristotle *Ethics* 6. 2. 1139a21, trans. W. D. Ross: "What affirmation and negation are in thinking, pursuit and avoidance are in desire; so that since moral virtue is a state of character concerned with choice, and choice is deliberate desire, therefore both the reasoning must be true and the desire right, if the choice is to be good, and the latter must pursue just what the former asserts. Now this kind of

truth is practical; of the intellect which is contemplative, not practical, not productive, the good and the bad state are truth and falsity respectively (for this is the work of everything intellectual); while of the part which is practical and intellectual the good state is truth in agreement with right desire." *Sum. theol.* i-ii. 57. 5 ad 3, trans. A. C. Pegis: "As is stated in *Ethics* vi., truth is not the same for the practical as for the speculative intellect. For the truth of the speculative intellect depends on the conformity of the intellect to the thing. And since the intellect cannot be infallibly in conformity with things in contingent matters, but only in necessary matters, therefore no speculative habit about contingent things is an intellectual virtue, but only such as is about necessary things.—On the other hand, the truth of the practical intellect depends on conformity with right appetite. This conformity has no place in necessary matters, which are not effected by the human will, but only in contingent matters which can be effected by us, whether they be matters of interior action or the products of external work. Hence it is only about contingent matters that an intellectual virtue is assigned to the practical intellect, viz., *art*, as regards things to be made, and *prudence* as regards things to be done."

13. Thomas Aquinas *Com. in Eth. II*, les. 2, trans. Thomas Gilby: "Disquisitions on general morality are not entirely trustworthy, and the ground becomes more uncertain when one wishes to descend to individual cases in detail. The factors are infinitely variable, and cannot be settled whether by art or precedent. Judgment should be left to the people concerned. Each must set himself to act according to the immediate situation and the circumstances involved. The decision may be unerring in the concrete, despite the uneasy debate in the abstract. Nevertheless, the moralist can provide some help and direction in such cases."

14. The relevant texts are: Aristotle *Ethics* 10. 5. 1176a17; Thomas Aquinas *Sum. theol.* i. 1. 6 ad 3; i-ii. 65. 1, 2; 95. 2 ad 4; ii-ii. 45. 2; John of St. Thomas *Cursus theologicus* i-ii, disp. 18, a. 4, ([Paris: Vivès, 1885], VI, 634 ff.); J. Maritain, *Reflexions sur l'intelligence* (Paris: Nouvelle librairie nationale, 1924), pp. 88 and 110 ff.

15. *Sum. theol.* i. 2. 3. See also J. Maritain, *Approaches to God*, trans. Peter O'Reilly (New York: Harper and Brothers, 1954).

16. The use of the terms "proof" and "demonstration" in this context calls for a comment. We may borrow Maritain's explanation. Remarking that Thomas Aquinas preferred to use the word "ways," Maritain writes: "Our arguments do not give us evidence of the divine existence itself or of the act of existing which is in God and which is God Himself—as if one could have the evidence of His existence without having that of His essence. They give us only evidence of the fact that the divine existence must be affirmed, or of

the truth of the attribution of the predicate to the subject in the assertion 'God exists.' In short, what we prove when we prove the existence
of God is something which infinitely surpasses us—us and our ideas
and our proofs. . . . [The] words 'proof' and 'demonstration,' in reference to the existence of God, must be understood (and in fact are
so understood spontaneously) with resonances other than in the current usage—in a sense no less strong as to their rational efficacy but
more modest in that which concerns us and more reverential in that
which concerns the object. On this condition it remains perfectly
legitimate to use them. It is just a matter of marking well the difference
in station. This being understood, we shall not hesitate to say 'proof'
or 'demonstration' as well as 'way,' for all these words are synonymous
in the sense we have just specified." *Approaches to God*, pp. 12, 13, 14.

17. *De aeternitate mundi* (1270-71); quoted in *Approaches to God*,
pp. 40-41n.

18. *Ibid.*, p. 23. As Maritain explains subsequently, the five ways
of Thomas Aquinas put forth in *Sum. theol.* i. 2.3., "lead of themselves to the existence of a First Being, the cause of all the others.
This is—at the stage of 'nominal definition' (but there is no *definition* of God)—what everyone understands by the word God. In the
following articles [of the *Summa*], where it is established that the first
Being is pure Act and that in Him essence and existence are strictly
identical, the proof is achieved and completed. At that moment, we
are able to see what it is that makes the First Being to be truly God,
what it is that properly characterizes that First Being as God, namely,
His infinite transcendence, and his essential and infinite distinction
from all other beings" (pp. 68-69).

19. *Ibid.*, pp. 69-70: "Although the creation and conservation of
things are one and the same action in God, they are distinct where
things are concerned. God *creates* things without using any intermediary—nothing created can serve as instrument for the creation of another thing (because an instrument disposes a pre-existing matter, and
there is here no pre-existing matter). But God *conserves* things in
being by employing as an intermediary cause the activity of agents,
themselves created, which concur instrumentally to maintain one
another in existence.

"It follows from this that if one considers the five ways as leading
to the First Cause insofar as it *conserves* things in being, the demonstration, proceeding from the axiom 'One cannot go on infinitely in
the series of causes,' envisages a series of causes superordinated to one
another which is really given as a matter of fact, although we might
be more or less at a loss to put our finger on each of these diverse
causes in particular. Besides, it suffices for our argument to make
them up as we please.

"But if the five ways are considered as leading to the First Cause insofar as it *creates* things in being, the demonstration, proceeding from the axiom 'One cannot go on infinitely in the series of causes' envisages a series of causes superordinated to one another which, as a matter of fact, is not really given. We may imagine these diverse causes as we please—they remain imaginary. They provide logical aid to the demonstration. We may suppose that they exist, and then it becomes clear that to rise from cause to cause endlessly is impossible. In reality, however, the First Cause to which one is thus led—the Cause which is beyond all possible series in the world of experience—is the only cause that causes in the sense of creating (causing things *ex nihilo*).

"For all that, it is clear that this very fact, that things are created, is only known by us once we know that the First Cause exists; consequently, we cannot make use of it in order to demonstrate the existence of that First Cause. All we know from the outset is that things are caused. And it is on the fact that they are caused (not on the fact that they are created, nor on the fact that they are conserved in being) that we take our stand in order to rise to the necessary existence of the First Cause—without as yet distinguishing between causation which conserves and causation which creates, but rather by prescinding from this distinction."

20. Merrit Hadden Moore, vol. III, no. 1, pp. 6-7.

21. (The following note and all the references to the works of Thomas Aquinas in this section are by Clifford G. Kossel, S.J., whose help is hereby gratefully acknowledged. Ed.) Although St. Thomas nowhere treats these matters in precisely this order, the principles and many of the examples used in this section are drawn from his writings. Of course, being a theologian St. Thomas was writing theological works (except for the commentaries on Aristotle), and so the materials on natural law are found within a general theological context. This may cause some initial difficulty for the non-theological reader, but it does not alter the clarity and precision of St. Thomas's thought on these matters. The more important passages relevant to this section are the following. The general principles of the stability and variability of natural law are best treated in *Sum. theol.* i-ii, 94, aa. 4-6. Some helpful clarifications and many examples are contained in the treatise on the Old (Mosaic) Law, i-ii, 100. The nature and kinds of circumstances which affect the human act are treated in i-ii, 7. The effect of circumstances on the morality of actions is detailed throughout the treatise on the morality of human acts, i-ii, aa. 18-20, and in the *De Malo*, q. 2, especially aa. 4-7. Some matter from the treatise on law is repeated but in more detail and from a different aspect in the treatise on justice in *Sum theol.* ii-ii. Cf. especially qq. 57 (nature and kinds

of rights), 58 (nature of justice), 61 (on the two species of justice, distributive and commutative), 54 (duties with regard to human life), 66 (private property), 78 (usury), 120 (equity).

CHAPTER 6

1. *Jean-Jacques Rousseau et la science politique de son temps* (Paris: Presses universitaires de France, 1950).

2. *Theodore Roosevelt: An Autobiography* (New York: Charles Scribner's Sons, 1908), 470-71.

3. The statement is attributed to a president of a railroad company in 1900 in S. E. Morrison and H. S. Commager, *The Growth of the American Republic* (New York: Oxford University Press, 1942), vol. II, p. 164.

Index

Abstraction, mathematical, 48, 75
Adultery, 152
Alms, 149
American Revolution, 8, 120
Analogy, kinds of, 69-70 n.; of proper proportionality, 110-111
Aquinas, on animal intelligence, 182 n. 7; on definition of law, 71, 109; on divine will, 34; on divisions of natural law, 122ff.; on moral premises, 186 n. 13; on practical truth, 186 n. 12; on distinction between art and prudence, 183 n. 14; on universals, 168 n. 4
Archimedes, 43
Aristotle, 3, 5, 75; on animal intelligence, 81; on chance, 59; death of, 28, 31; on definition, 70-71; on dialectic method, 13, 20, 170 n. 7; on God, 27-28, 142, 175 n. 13; influence on American slavery ideology, 171 n. 2; on manual labor, 29, 81; on nature, 41, 42, 44, 44-45 n.; on natural law, 27ff., 131, 167 n. 2; on Parmenides, 45-46; on plurality of natures, 45; on practical truth, 185 n. 12; on transitive and immanent actions, 183 n. 15; on universals, 7, 168 n. 4

Antigone, 131
Art, political, 92ff.
Austro-Hungarian Empire, 9
Authority, contrasted with law, 83-84
Axiom, meaning of, 63-64, 77; in mathematics, 75, 134

Beauvoir, Simone de, 123
Bellarmine, 160
Bergson, Henri, 12, 33, 169 n. 6; on open society, 31, 175 n. 16
Bodin, 62, 72
Bolyai, 43
Bonald, de, 54, 178 n. 12
Broglie, Louis de, 57, 180 n. 18

Calhoun, John C., on slavery, 17, 170 n. 1, 171 n. 2
Cause, first, 141ff.; plurality of causes, 55
Channing, W. E., 103-105, 184 n. 16
Cognition, definition of, 21
Collective bargaining, 164
Communist Manifesto, 98
Comte, Auguste, 19, 172 n. 3
Concordia Discordantium Canonum, 32

191